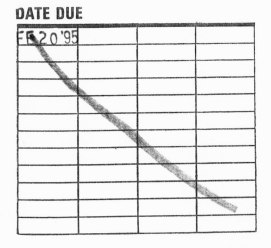

Choices

Public Education for the 21st Century

Don L. Fuhr
Educational Administration
Clemson University
Clemson, South Carolina

UNIVERSITY
PRESS OF
AMERICA

Lanham • New York • London

Copyright © 1990 by
University Press of America®, Inc.
4720 Boston Way
Lanham, Maryland 20706

3 Henrietta Street
London WC2E 8LU England

Library of Congress Cataloging-in-Publication Data

Fuhr, Don L., 1934—
Choices : public education for the 21st century / Don L. Fuhr.
p.   cm.
Includes bibliographical references
1. Education—United States.
I. Title.
LA212.F8   1990   370'.973—dc20   90–38140 CIP

ISBN 0–8191–7879–9 (alk. paper)
ISBN 0–8191–7880–2 (pbk. : alk. paper)

Acknowledgements

All books are collaborative efforts, for our
thoughts and beliefs come from those who influence our
lives. I thank my many colleagues in the field who
have enlarged and clarified my perceptions and insights
regarding the modern-day world of public education.

It is difficult to single out those who have
contributed to the completion of this work. However,
this book became a reality due to the dedication and
shared commitment of Joyce Farr who provided her
clerical talents, energy, and support to keep things
moving along from beginning to end.

My gratitude goes to Elaine Lesley who contributed
her editing skills and suggestions throughout the manu-
script. My deep gratitude is especially extended to
John Wade, principal of Edwards Junior High (selected
as one of the outstanding junior high schools in the
country in 1989), who served as a sounding board for
many of the ideas and practices suggested in the
following pages.

My thanks also go to the following individuals:
Kathy Brazinski, Joel Evans, and Mark Rowe who in one
way or another contributed their ideas and time towards
the completion of this book.

I extend my gratitude and deep appreciation to my
mother, Ruthie (who at ninety-one can carry on a lively
discussion on any topic), for her love, discipline and
advice along the way; to my late father who taught me
dedication and hard work pays off; and to my three
children - Janet, Donna, and Mark - who made parenting
a joy and an honor.

Most of all, I am grateful to my wife, Annie, who was always there when I needed her--reading and motivating me to keep plowing ahead. Her unselfish giving and love helped bring this project to completion.

Most of the single-page quotes were taken from a special edition of <u>Business Week</u> magazine by Dennis P. Doyle, 1989, pp. E4 - E122, entitled <u>Endangered Species: Children of Promise</u>.

Contents

Preface

Legend has it that long ago and far away there lived a kind, loving and much respected wise man. In the same land was a rich prince who hated the wise man. He saw the wise man taking from him the love of the people. The people listened to the wise man but not the prince and that angered the prince beyond belief. One day the prince said to his followers, "I have a plan whereby I can discredit the wise man - a way in which I can make him appear to be a fool. Each day the wise man goes to the market place where he speaks to people and gives them advice. Tomorrow I will go as a peasant. In my hand, I shall hold a white dove. When the crowd has gathered, I will raise my voice and say, 'Wise man, I have a simple question. This dove that I hold in my hand, is it alive or dead?' If he says alive, I will crush the bird in my hand and let it fall dead to the ground. If he says dead, I will open my hand and let the bird fly away. This surely will discredit the old man and the people will once again turn to me."

The next day as the crowd gathered in the market place, the rich prince, dressed as a peasant, waited until the crowd gathered and then he shouted, "Wise man, I would ask a simple question. This dove which I hold in my hand, is it alive or dead?" The crowd grew quiet and all eyes turned toward the wise man. The wise man paused, then looked at the prince disguised as a peasant, and said, "That which you hold in your hand, it is ... what you make of it. The choice is yours" (Mamchak, 1983).

The American people have the "dove of public education" in their collective hands, and they have the power to make the necessary changes. They too need to know what the problems are before they can make intell-

igent choices about the kind of schools they want for
their community.   This book will present certain information that may be common knowledge for those employed
by school districts, but not well known by the people
they serve. The goal is to present current issues
confronting public education, to submit some practical
suggestions on how to handle these pressing issues, to
motivate the readers (taxpayers) to get involved by
actually acquainting themselves with the needs of their
schools, and to make the necessary choices to raise the
standards in their own community schools. As with the
dove, we can choose to support and upgrade our public
school systems and watch them soar to great heights; or
we can choose to keep a tight grip, resisting needed
change, and watch our schools slowly decay.

There are many excellent books and articles published proclaiming the need for upgrading our schools.
Television and newspapers offer get-smart-quick reme-
dies for students who desire to improve their test
scores. New curriculum packages are offered every year
in valiant hope to stimulate both the teacher and the
student. Educational reform packages call for extending the school year with more time being devoted to the
teaching of reading, writing and arithmetic. Everyone
is jumping up and down over the concern for public
education in this country, but very few are moving
ahead. The improvement that needs to take place in
public education will come from the choices that are
made in the next few years. The responsibility for
those choices and changes are in the hands of every
taxpayer; most specifically, the parents of the
students in the classrooms.

Some communities have seen what is happening
nationally: an ever-increasing dropout rate, schools
producing graduates who are ill prepared and unable to
take over the reins of a new century with its new
demands. They are getting involved in their schools;
volunteering their time to act as teacher aides; do-
nating needed visual aids, computers, equipment; and,
most importantly, supporting their children's teachers
and school administrators. For some communities, the
reverse is true. In spite of all the books that have
been written crying for reform and all the protests of
overburdened teachers, much of the public still has the

attitude, "well, good ol' P.S. 41 was good enough for
me, it's good enough for my kids." The fact is, folks,
that what we learned in the classroom twenty years ago
will not prepare our children today for the demanding,
high-tech jobs in this computer-oriented world. Everyone is aware of the fact that the outside pressures -
changes in the culture, the impact of single-parenting,
drugs, latch-key kids - have tremendous impact on what
happens inside the school. Throwing money at the
problems will not make them go away. There are some
basic changes and choices that must be made not only to
prepare our children for their future jobs, but to
instill in them a love for learning, a respect for
their teachers, a desire to grow intellectually through
all of their lives, and a longing to know more.

I must say at the outset that there are many, many
quality schools in this country with outstanding leadership, tremendous community support, and enthusiastic
teachers and students. The problem is that this is not
the norm. What do these "ideal" school systems do that
make them work where other schools fail? The one thing
that the thriving, healthy schools have in common
regardless of where they are located or the amount of
resources that are available, is strong, effective,
assertive leadership at the top combined with the
respect and visible support of the community. To the
taxpayers it means consciously making the choice to
learn what's happening in their schools today and then
choosing to make a commitment to support the endeavors
that lead to educational excellence as we near the
beginning of the 21st century.

It is my hope that this book informs you, the
reader, about what is going on in public education
today. It is my goal that after reading, you will
choose to hold the dove in your hand and help set it
aloft in order that our public schools will soar to
greater heights.

Chapter 1

The Challenges of Public Education: How Extensive Are They?

*"Just as it is necessary for individuals to accept
and even welcome challenges to their maps of
reality and modi operandi if they are to grow in
wisdom and effectiveness, so it is necessary for
organizations to accept and welcome challenges
if they are to be viable and progressive
institutions."*

--M. Scott Peck
The Road Less Traveled

Public education is big business. During the
school year 1988-89, 40.2 million students were enrolled in elementary and secondary schools in the
United States. The average spending for each student
in public elementary and secondary schools has improved, rising from $3,988 per child in 1986-87 to
$4,509 during the 1988-89 school year. Total expen-
ditures for elementary and secondary education, including capital outlay and interest, accounted for
185.9 billion dollars in 1988-89. With an estimated
instructional staff of more than 2.6 million (classroom
teachers, non-supervisory instructional staff, principals and supervisors), effective management at local,
state, and national levels of public education becomes
an enormous challenge (Data Search, 1989).

The second challenge facing leaders of our present
day public schools involves funding. There is no
question that inadequate funding has hurt public edu-

cation. State and federal governments have played political games at the expense, rather than the benefit, of public education. This country spends twenty times more annually to keep a person in prison than it does to educate a student in our public schools. To achieve a better product in public education, we must be willing to pay for what it costs to hire good administrators and teachers. Marc Tucker, executive director of the Carnegie Forum on Education and the Economy, stated, "If we're going to be competitive, it's going to cost more." Tucker's recommendation calls for a 50-percent increase in teachers' salaries bringing the average up to $35,000 a year. This increase would make public school teachers in the United States stand slightly above that of Japanese teachers. The average public school teacher's salary (1988-89) in the United States is $29,567 (Data Search, 1989, pp. 1-10); and experts, such as economist Lester Thurow, are predicting that it will take $20 billion to raise teacher salaries $10,000 a year. Thurow states, "Talking about raising teacher standards without raising wages is to talk about the impossible. In a capitalist economy, Americans get the quality that they are willing to pay for" (Education Week, 24 July 1987, p. 14).

The third challenge facing our elementary and secondary schools involves the present-day responsibilities of the school administrator. No longer are school administrators looked upon as those with easy jobs. Administrators are faced with ever-changing "issues of the day" which involve more and more demands on their time. Some of us can remember the day when our principal or superintendent could walk into the classroom and not a sound was heard. Gone are the days when school administrators had total support and respect without outside interference from the community and special interest groups. In comparison to present times, the education profession in the early and mid-twentieth century was a protected position for school administrators. State and federal governments had not yet invented the modern bureaucratic machine, so school administrators enjoyed opening school in the fall and closing it in the spring without the hassle of insurmountable meetings, paper work, and work stoppages. The scene has changed drastically. I am not aware of any other group of management personnel in private or public sectors that has had a more radical change in responsibilities and duties than public school administrators. The problems connected with this rapidly changing role for public school management personnel are compounded by sub-par salaries and a lack of training to cope with the societal changes that affect public education. Although more will be said about school administrators in Chapter 2, let us briefly take a look at one aspect of school administration, the position of superintendent of schools in the United States today.

The average length of service for a superintendent of schools in a large urban school system (50,000 plus student population) in this country is slightly more than four years. The job of superintendent of schools is a perilous position. An increasing number of superintendents annually search for top-level positions in other school systems primarily because they trust a new location will offer added stability and security over their present position.

The fact is, the system cannot build a solid management team to lead an organization such as a public school system when top level administrators only stay long enough to discover the streets that lead to each school in their district. Until recently, certain school districts in Georgia and South Carolina, for example, selected their local school superintendent by popular vote. In one Georgia district, the grand jury appointed the school board members and every four years the superintendent was, and still is elected by popular vote. As a result, the position of superintendent of schools in such districts is shaky. One can easily see how "playing politics" might take precedence over effective management. For many, July 1 each year signals the changing of the guard. Some school boards offer only a one-year contract to their new superintendent so they can assess performance for one year vs. granting a three-year term. If they don't like what they see at the end of one year, the recently hired superintendent is out and the search is on again. Accountable leadership cannot exist in our public school systems when there is constant mobility on the part of chief school executives.

The fourth challenge facing public education today relates to the largest professional group in this country - public school teachers. Walk into any elementary or secondary classroom today, and you will immediately understand the challenges facing teachers. Teachers are torn between attempting to cope with behavioral problems facing modern-day youth on one hand, while on the other, attempting to motivate them to learn in order to meet state mandated achievement requirements. Teaching is a demanding profession, and the outcry is for less bureaucratic paperwork and more time to teach. Teachers from rural, suburban and urban school districts are constantly in search of materials and programs that will work in their classrooms enabling them to deal with monumental social changes.

Consider these findings that appeared in the Principal, January 1986, a monthly publication of the National Association of Elementary School Principals, about today's children:

- 14 percent are illegitimate
- 40 percent will be living with a single parent by their eighteenth birthday
- 30 percent are "latchkey" children
- 20 percent live in poverty
- 15 percent speak another language
- 15 percent have physical or mental handicaps
- 10 percent have poorly educated parents.

Many teachers who teach under these conditions can do little more than maintain order in the classroom. The end result is a bogged-down educational system, which is unable to meet the needs of students who must be prepared for a new century of living.

The fifth challenge facing public education relates to the top governing body of public school systems: school boards. The primary responsibility of a board of education is (1) to formulate policies and (2) to see that the policies are implemented within the school district. However, with the enormous complexities of public education today, school boards in this country are constantly searching for ways to cope with the governing of their respective school districts.

"If I've learned one thing,
it's that the answer to
virtually all our national
problems--from
international competitiveness
to improving our standard
of living to the very
security of our nation--
ultimately rests on
one word ...'education'."
                    --Robert D. Kirkpatrick,
                    Chairman, CIGNA

For example, in November 1983, the majority of school districts in Illinois (1011 total school districts) had a minimum of four seats out of a total seven-member board up for re-election. The final outcome of the elections caused many changes to occur in school systems throughout the state. Superintendents were dismissed, division existed among old and new board members, and politics dominated local school districts more than anytime in the history of the state. In addition, teacher unions became stronger in the state during this same period primarily because the governor signed a collective bargaining bill which granted public employees the right to strike. Therefore, the need for school boards to cope with the rapidly changing times of public education by incorporating modern day practices of positive management techniques infused with future planning and goal-oriented self-evaluations of their individual performances is a must. Failure to incorporate such management procedures by boards of education will cause school systems to decay rapidly.

The sixth challenge facing public education today involves our administrator and teacher training institutions. Dr. Derek Bok, President of Harvard University, in his 1985-86 address to the members of the Board of Overseers at the University, stated the following regarding educational training institutions:

> Few undertakings in higher education have been so consistently maligned and generations of effort have failed to produce any persuasive evidence that formal training produces more effective instructors. Still it is hard to imagine how a professional school of education can fail to include some program for training those who stand in front of the young....unless education faculties accept this challenge they will turn their backs on a problem of central importance to the profession they are meant to serve.

The image and quality of many of our teacher training institutions throughout this country are below par. Keep in mind the teaching profession is the foundation upon which all other professions have their origin. But the practice of teaching is generally looked upon as a second-rate profession by the public as well as other professions. We are not attracting the "best" into our education schools primarily because of low salaries and lack of accountability within the present structure. There is a demanding need to salvage what is good and build toward a new vision of accountability as well as respectability. In order to meet this need, many school districts and administrator/teacher training institutions are two separate entities in this country.

The seventh challenge involves special self-interest groups within school districts who crusade for any topic imaginable in order to gain control of decision and policy making. Their motives are often selfish compared to common interest groups who attempt to consider the needs of the majority. Special self-interest groups have been forming at an alarming rate throughout the majority of school districts across our country. Their influence is especially felt during the selection of school board members, the removal of school board members, and the hiring or the dismissal of superintendents.

During my administrative years attending Board of Education meetings, the following sample of statements, recommendations, and questions were brought up by special self-interest groups resulting in lively, but not necessarily healthy, debates between school officials and the public:

1. Why doesn't the school district food program include chunky peanut butter in the student's sandwiches?
2. The superintendent should be more careful in selecting his "fishing buddies."
3. It's time to fire the superintendent because having been in the district for six years he has outlived his usefulness.
4. To show their support for those who attend board meetings, a snack should be served to the public by the Board of Education.
5. There should be more emphasis at the junior

and senior high schools to show girls how to not have babies as well as how to have them!

6. There should be included in the senior high physical education program the fundamental exercise program patterned after marine boot camp training.

7. Teachers should be paid more than administrators.

8. Administrators should fire more teachers.

9. The superintendent should be more visible.

10. Why do certain board members frequently visit a local bar after each board meeting?

For many years, faced with similar questions and items, school administrators and board of education members have been over-responding and over-reacting when special self-interest groups have demanded special concessions from the school. This can cause excessive division of the educational program in any school district. In some cases, special interests have overtaken the common interests concerning the education of the child. This weakens the foundation upon which education is built within any school district. Public education has been listening too much to the special interest groups and not enough to its own conscience and the broader public mandate of public education. This is not to condemn public input. Certainly legitimate concerns and issues need to be brought before boards of education to enable superintendents or presidents of the board of education to be aware of all the major happenings or events taking place in their school district. However, the board of education and the superintendent must provide leadership and proper organization to allow people to be heard but not to take over.

The eighth challenge of public education today, and one of major concern, especially to school administrators, is the bureaucratic machine. The common joke told many times by experienced front-line administrators is the one where an "old time" superintendent tells a new principal: "Do you know what the three greatest lies in the world are?" "No," said the new principal. The "old time" veteran superintendent said, "(1) Let's stop and have one beer, (2) Your paycheck is in the mail, and (3) I am from the

State Board of Education and I am here to help you!"
Much of the support school districts receive from state
and federal governments is accompanied by bureaucratic
paperwork.   It seems as though State Boards of Education, especially, have to ask for ever-increasing
reports to verify and justify each department's
existence.

Top-level public school administrators (or teachers, for that matter) state that their paperwork has
tripled in the last decade, primarily because of state
and federal mandates.   More reports require the hiring
of more personnel which results in more expenditures.
The sad commentary among many front-line school administrators is that, despite the time and energy that
goes into completing many reports at the local school
level, they are often not read.   I can remember once
signing a student minority form whereby we deliberately
listed 25 percent of our student body as Eskimos.   I
wanted to see if anyone at the state level read the
report.   It took hours to complete the form because of
many individual columns wanting information on every
minority student by school, grade, age, and sex.   The
report when completed was not tied to funding, and we
questioned seriously if anyone read the thing.
Evidently no one did.   No one ever questioned the existence of an Eskimo colony in the Midwest!

The Lau decision of several years ago provides
another example of federal red tape.   The Lau case
involved mandated bilingual education for students
whose native language was something other than English.
When the Lau decision was made, the law contained 375
words.   When the Lau regulations were written, it
contained 4,400.   The increase in verbiage, according
to the American Association of School Administrators,
is just one of the problems which has arisen between
school districts and the regulatory agencies of
government (AASA Convention Reporter, 13 February 1981,
p. 7).

The hot lunch program offers still another good
example of paper bureaucracy.   The current trend in
many school districts is to turn the food program over
to outside food vendors.   With the money squeeze
hitting many districts, it is often cheaper, without

"We need to adopt that
famous Noah principle:
No more prizes
for predicting rain.
Prizes only for
building arks."
--Louis V. Gerstner, CEO
RJR/Nabisco.

sacrificing quality, to enter into a contract with a food vendor. However, another major reason for switching over to outside vendors has been the increasing number of reports that must be filed with government agencies. Because of the confusion over figuring direct and indirect costs that are charged to the program, school lunch programs rank among the top in paperwork confusion.

Attempting to meet these never-ending predictable challenges makes life interesting enough for most school administrators. Today, they are faced with more and more unpredictable challenges. I have served in school administration from the assistant principal level up through, and including, superintendent of schools. I have been a witness to, as well as directly involved in, strikes by teachers, shootings of teachers (by students), teachers assaults on students, and even leaving a child on the bus, believe it or not! But the one incident that I remember most dates back to 1978 when I decided to accept the position of superintendent of schools in Aurora, Illinois.

I came to Aurora from the Upper Darby School System in Upper Darby, Pennsylvania, a medium size, upper middle income district situated adjacent to Philadelphia where I served as an assistant superintendent for five years. While serving in the Pennsylvania district, instructional happenings and advancements occurred which built a good basis for my marketability to seek a superintendent's position. Admittedly, there were times sitting around board of education meetings until 1:00 and 2:00 a.m. that I thought seeking a superintendency was only for those individuals who didn't know better. However, in the spring of 1978, the placement office at the University of Pittsburg contacted me wanting to know if I would be interested in a superintendent's position in Aurora, Illinois. After several days deliberation, I decided to apply. The worst thing that could happen would be that I wouldn't get the job, and I would continue in my present job. After several meetings with the Aurora East Board of Education, they offered me the position.

In August 1978, I officially assumed the superintendency. I asked the school board to state their

number one priority. They informed me they wanted the
school system to move "forward." After a year on the
job, I decided to "rock the boat" in order to make
things happen. (An old fishing buddy of mine used to
say, "Make sure you're real comfortable in the saddle
before you stick in the spurs.") The school district's
minority population at the time was approximately 55%.
In addition, there were some unique characteristics
about this Illinois school system. For example, there
was no busing of students since a lawsuit filed by the
board of education was pending against the Illinois
State Board of Education over the issue of school
desegregation at the time. The main controversy was
whether or not the Illinois Department of Education had
the power to force busing upon a school district, or
was such power and duties under the jurisdiction of the
state legislature? The case was finally decided by the
Illinois Supreme Court who ruled in favor of the school
district stating only the state legislature has a right
to require busing through policy adoption. No one
wanted busing--not the parents, not the board of education, not the staff. The State Board of Education felt
minority students in the school district were being
cheated in their education since certain schools had
larger or smaller student minority enrollments than
others.

Also unique to the Aurora East District at the
time I became superintendent was the absence of a
teachers' union. No bargaining took place between the
teachers and the board of education. Teachers were
issued individual contracts with salary increases and
benefits determined solely by the board of education.

Finally, the school district was debt free. All
debts were paid, with a tax rate that was the lowest in
the county. With a stable and solid board of education
behind me, things started to move forward in the school
district. Student achievement scores increased, revised staff evaluation procedures were instituted
(merit pay based on performance objectives), and a
five-year long-range plan was started. Student attendance increased and a public relations program was
implemented that focused on bringing key community
leaders and management personnel into the school district for first-hand inspection and support. There was

increased parental involvement. Residing business partnerships were formed and a nationally recognized "Up With Achievement" program, designed to excite students to learn, was launched in 1981 with great success. All in all, things were going well in this Illinois school district. My personal management philosophy was one of delegating, motivating and evaluating, which in this school district resulted in a vision shared by a dedicated staff who wanted the best for the school district.

Then, in 1982, things of a different nature started to occur in the school district. The financial well started to run dry. With no local tax base to draw upon, plus rising inflation and drastic cutbacks in state funding, the debt-free Aurora East School District was being faced with dire consequences. In addition, major industrial companies had either left town or closed down.

As the 1983-84 budget year was being planned, I asked the board of education the following question at a December board meeting. "Do you want to maintain a balanced budget or begin a deficit one?" The board responded with a unanimous vote for a balanced budget, which was no surprise, based on the history of the school district being debt free for so many years. To arrive at a balanced budget, drastic cuts would have to be made, and I was responsible for presenting the plan that would result in a balanced budget. To accomplish the assignment, I presented the following recommendations before a packed house at a public meeting:

- 189 teaching positions to be eliminated
- All extra-curricular activities to be eliminated at the junior and senior high levels, including all varsity and junior high sports
- Art and music programs to be eliminated at the elementary levels
- Maintenance repairs to be halted; only emergency repairs would be authorized
- All administrative and teacher salaries to be frozen including salary step increases
- Travel and convention funds to be frozen
- Supply budgets to be cut by 25%.

"Judge a leader's
ability by the size
of the problems
he tackles."

If a school district needs some press coverage and attention, I guarantee recommending approval on the items listed above will do it. After many meetings and discussions, the board of education finally approved my recommendations. As a result of such action, on March 29, 1983, Chicago television stations were calling as soon as I arrived at my office wanting to know if there was going to be a walkout by students protesting the dismissing of teachers and the elimination of sports and extra-curricular activities within the school district. I responded, in all honesty, that I wasn't aware of any such thing happening, but was soon to discover that I was dead wrong. Immediately following the phone inquiries, one of our high school principals called me at 8:30 a.m. and said, "Doc, they're walking out on me over here, and I can't get them back in. What should I do?"

I asked, "Where are they going?"

He replied, "They're coming over to see you!"

I responded by saying, "I'll head them off at the pass as they come down 5th Avenue." This particular high school at the time had an enrollment of 1,600 students. After the students left the school, the enrollment dropped from 1600 to 4, which included my son, his girlfriend, and two school board members' children. The march was officially on! Time was of importance so I immediately appointed a command guard (administrative personnel and secretaries) to station themselves at the administration building parking lot, rear and front doors, on the roof and at all four corners of the building. As we waited for the marchers, I started to understand how General George Custer might have felt at the Little Big Horn.

While we waited for the visible signs that the students were coming, we soon were told they decided to march up to the nearby junior high school and were attempting to get those students (enrollment 1,000) to join in the march, which they did. Now there was a full-fledge regiment of students marching toward their destination, the Central Administration Building of the Aurora East School District. Prior to their arrival, the media brigade arrived with cameras and TV anchor personalities and reporters as well as the police and hundreds of curious onlookers. The showdown was soon to begin.

Finally, we heard them shouting: "We want Sports
Back," "Give Us Back Our Teachers," "Down with the
Board   of   Education   and   Superintendent."   As   the
marchers   drew   near,   I   was   thinking   back   on   what
graduate course in educational administration I could
recall that would give me a clue as to what to do.
Finally, unable to recall any such course, I decided to
pray.   Time was running out.   It was futile to try to
talk   over   the   shouting   and   yelling   coupled   with
television miocrophones and cameras all around my face.
The thought then occurred to me to enlist the support
of student leaders.   From the crowd, I picked the state
wrestling   champion,   the   star   basketball   player,   the
football captain and anyone else who was over six feet
tall   to   assist   me   in   quieting   the   crowd.   They   came
forward and, believe it or not, the plan worked.   "Keep
quiet, let 'Doc' speak.   Keep your mouth shut so we can
hear what the Superintendent has to tell us."   I now
have even a greater respect for making decisions based
on intuition and "gut" feelings.

With TV cameras and microphones in my face, I told
the crowd of students, who by this time were in tree
tops and on the roof of the administration building,
that I would do everything possible to secure enough
funds to reinstate educational staff and the programs
that were cut, but I needed the support of the community, including their parents.   "Trust in me, that is
all I request."   Then I told them I wanted to meet with
five   representatives   from   the   student   council.   I
instructed   the   wrestling   champion,   basketball   and
football captains, plus a few others to quiet the crowd
and to lead the gathering back to their schools.
Again, it worked!   Within 30 minutes, the majority of
the students were back in their respective schools.
The TV people were very disappointed because they
assumed there was going to be a full-fledged riot, but
not a shot was fired.   Phone calls came in from all
over the Midwest.   Wire services were calling wanting
to know the details about the stabbings that took
place, about the police having to take students to the
hospital, and about the thousands of dollars in property damage.   Nothing of the sort had happened.   The day
ended calmly and peacefully.

There were negative and positive outcomes from the

"Being able to
accept criticism
makes you a prime
candidate for the
Wise-Man's
Hall of Fame."

incident. After several months of financial uncer-
tainty, the state legislature came forth with necessary
funds for our district which enabled the call-back of
some 130 teachers and other non-certified personnel in
the school district. Sports programs were restored on
a voluntary basis with volunteer organizations kicking
in some $20,000 to keep a year of athletics going at
the senior high school. Parents united and got involved, physically and financially, to keep the school
district's extra curricular programs from being
abolished.

The final scene of all of this was presented at
the November election where thirteen candidates ran for
five seats on the board of education. Several of the
original members of the board decided not to seek
re-election when their term was up. Several others ran
and were defeated. The outcome was the election of a
new majority to the board of education.

All of these events basically occurred because I
asked the board one basic question: Do you want a
balanced budget or a deficit budget? This particular
event that occurred in the Illinois school district is
not unique. Similar events are occurring today in
school districts throughout the country. The cry for
more money as well as other critical needs is being
heard from all corners of public education. Many
districts in this country are unable to do an adequate
job of long range fiscal planning since school funding
is primarily at the mercy each year of state governments. Consequently, no one knows from year to year
what will happen.

So the challenges in public education keep rolling
in as consistently as the high tide on an ocean. The
concerns and problems that challenge today's school
officials, regardless of the size of the school district, are basically the same, only magnified many
times over in our larger systems. Once the school
doors open in the fall, the mission of educating our
youth begins. From the one-room schools in the Northwest to the comprehensive high schools in some of our
major cities and suburbs, paid professionals strive to
offer an educational "package" against overwhelming
odds.

Choices need to be made and addressed before the road to substantial recovery can begin in public education. Choices must be made based on familiarity with the product of public education in order to keep us on the road of accountability. I join with the others who have been "in the trenches" and believe that students don't determine the quality of education taking place in our schools, regardless of whether they come from low income homes, broken homes, single-parent homes, or well-to-do homes. What determines the quality of education in our schools are the paid professionals with the support of the parents and community. It is my belief that public schools can work at providing a quality education for the students. If they don't, then school officials should find out why and make the necessary changes.

Our fast-approaching 21st century is one that will present a new host of challenges for our public schools. Only by having our schools working in an accountable fashion will public education move forward to meet these challenges.

Chapter 2

Can Administrators Administrate?

"Decisions: Men grow making decisions and assuming responsibility for them."

--Robert O'Brien
Marriott

Can administrators administrate? The word admin-istrate, in relation to public schools, involves two areas: management and leadership. Management relates to carrying out the required daily duties of operating a particular school or school district. Meeting certi-fication requirements, completing reports, conducting fire drills, maintaining a clean school, ordering supplies and carrying out mandated district, state and federal policies--all of these relate to management responsibilities. Leadership, on the other hand, in-volves going beyond the daily routine of seeing that things get done. Taking chances, plotting a vision, handling the unexpected, implementing skillful human relation strategies, turning failures into successes-- all of these are trademarks of good leadership.

While carrying out management responsibilities is a must for all school administrators, the local community must make a choice: After giving them support and the flexibility to administrate, are we satisfied with the present corps of school administra-tors or should we choose to appoint and retain only those individuals who demonstrate profiles of success-ful leadership? In order for schools to improve, we cannot settle for administrators who can only manage. We must choose those who possess outstanding leadership skills.

The local taxpayers of any school system, be it rural, suburban or urban, often are not presented with enough information in order to support their choice for school administrator. The friends of friends, the "good ol' boys," and the family names - these factors have influenced voters in the past. The public must take it upon themselves to assume the responsibility of knowing who is going to pilot their child's school "ship" and voicing opinions on those choices. For example, the public needs to know that principals can determine whether or not teachers will teach with enthusiasm and dedication.

Failing to address the need for quality leadership in the governance of our public schools is like going fishing without any bait: Nothing occurs at the other end of the hook except snags, frustration and despair. Without quality leadership in our public schools, nothing occurs toward achieving desired outcomes, and students in this type of school environment fall prey to frustration, despair and apathy. They see no evidence of high expectations demanded for their role models (teachers) and consistently observe, for approximately 180 school days out of every year, many professionals "going through the motions" of teaching and administrating.

School administrators are the sparkplugs that make the school building move or not move towards educational excellence. Their leadership qualities determine the success of any school or school district. Without strong leadership, schools become places where routine and boredom set the climate in which our children are supposed to get excited about learning. A successful and effective principal, in tune with the times and needs of teachers and students, can create the positive, enthusiastic atmosphere that is conducive to learning.

The choice for the local public and supporters of public education must be to decide if they desire competent leadership at the helm of their respective elementary, middle and secondary schools.

The choice to have capable assistant principals, principals, assistant superintendents, and superintendents, etc., is a challenging one. Information must be provided to those in charge of selecting school administrators to equip them with knowledge and understanding of the qualities of leadership as well as what it takes to preserve it.

There are many competent administrators in public education today who effectively combine leadership with vision. They are addressing present happenings, and also targeting where they want to be in the future. Unfortunately, the situation in school administration today is that even the good school administrators can be caught up in the rapid turnover of top-level positions in school districts. In the superintendency, some are "hired to be fired." Administrators with top level positions in school districts throughout this country, who weather the storm of dealing with special self-interest groups, unionism, curtailment of funds, and board of education games, earn every bit of the salary they are paid.

Leadership in public education, as in the corporate world, has one main mission: to lead and build an organization effectively. The person in charge of a school district has to be a leader.

Many are asking the same question today: Why would anyone choose to be a superintendent of schools or principal when things are constantly churning in today's world of public education and the longevity rate for time spent in top-level administrative positions is so unstable? I believe today's practicing school administrators would say that they choose to be a school administrator because they:

(1) have the desire, willingness, and ability to lead an organization,
(2) feel satisfaction and fulfillment in addressing the challenges in today's world of public education,
(3) feel qualified to improve education for the betterment of children,
(4) desire to meet and work with people,
(5) desire increased salary and fringe benefits.

Even with a good intent to lead, school administrators, especially school superintendents, are caught in a no-win situation. Many understand their position as chief executive officer of a public school system to that of what some management experts brand as a "roller-coaster career": A career marked with national recognition and local criticism, educational accomplishments and personal failures.

Unless more stability is incorporated into the position of superintendent of schools, one must question seriously the choice to hire chief school executives. Too often, board of education members ignore or fail to understand the role of the superintendency. According to the board, this role involves seeing that the policies established by the local board of education and the state legislature are carried out in the school district. There are school districts where board members play superintendent as well as school board, and the end result is eventually turmoil and dissention. The superintendency in some school systems is becoming nothing more than a figurehead position. It is true some superintendents create such a situation through their own lack of leadership. They don't rock the boat for fear of getting fired. They spend the majority of their time putting out political grassfires, subsequently offering little in the way of direction or future planning. Such individuals are usually so insecure about their jobs that they would rather avoid making decisions than offending anyone.

I jokingly mention from time to time that, during the months of March, April, May, June and early July of each year, if one listens closely, one may hear the migration of superintendents in the quiet skies above. These months are the key times that many top-level school administrators hurry about the country, most in secret, looking for new positions. Canadian geese migrate north and south in the spring and fall; school administrators migrate north, east, south, and west on an average of five to six months every year. A constant change of top leadership personnel in many of our current school districts throughout the country is a serious threat to the health and welfare of the school system. The roots never take hold to sprout advancement. This non-leadership environment eventually fil-

> with faculty, support staff, board of
> education, community and students
> (4) Ability to communicate
> (5) Ability to establish and implement
> system-wide goals
> (6) Knowledge in personnel and financial
> management
> (7) Qualifies for state superintendent's
> certificate.

There are many qualified administrators in this country who meet the above requirements and can effectively administrate and lead a school or school district, but what happens? The newly-hired administrator discovers that although he is qualified, it's really the values and behavior of the school district community that determines whether there is a happy marriage or a future divorce in the making. Taxpayers must understand about the tax bill they are paying and what they are receiving in return, especially in the area of leadership. Once understood, taxpayers need to make a commitment to that leadership.

Having been a finalist or offered the position as superintendent in six school districts within a six-month period between February and June 1984, I kept the following scorecard. Incidentally, all six were nationally advertised positions so the competition was keen.

First: The scorecard on why the vacancy occurred was as follows:

Reason	# of Districts
Retirement	2
Contract not renewed	3
Resignation	1

Second: Various board members of each of the six districts were not sure how long they would remain as a member of the board of education.

Third: All six districts presently had financial problems or were anticipating reduction in state aid within the next year or two.

Fourth: Teacher negotiations varied among all six districts. Two districts issued individual teacher contracts, with little if any negotiating taking place; one had two teacher strikes over the last six years; consequently, negotiations were always intense.

Fifth: Salary and benefit packages among the six districts ranged from $52,000 to $75,000.

Sixth: Interview questions focused on qualifications with major emphasis on exploring board of education/superintendent relationships, followed by accomplishments and reasons for applying.

The last part of each interview allowed candidates to ask questions. I posed five basic questions to each board of education:

(1) What are the top three priorities in your school system?
(2) Where would you like to see the school system be five years from now?
(3) How do you perceive a successful superintendent/board of education working relationship?
(4) What two things can't you stand about a superintendent? (Ask this one at 11:30 p.m. after sitting around a board table for three or four hours).
(5) What evidence can you provide to illustrate how the board utilizes the team approach in addressing critical issues?

Those applying for administrative positions in today's public school systems must understand two things:

(1) QUALIFICATIONS ON PAPER ARE ONE THING AND ARE NOT NECESSARILY THE CRITERIA WHICH WILL LAND YOU THE POSITION.
(2) TRY YOUR BEST TO FIND OUT AS MUCH ABOUT THE SCHOOL DISTRICT AND THE BOARD OF EDUCATION BEFORE YOU SIGN ON THE DOTTED LINE.

Not to slight graduate school professors of school administration, but many education courses currently being used for certification of school administrators are of little practical use. Unfortunately, the emphasis is on the "why" (theory) and not the "how" (practical). Many college texts will help an aspiring school administrator develop theories, but we need more than theory; the emphasis needs to be directed towards strategy and practical expertise. Speaking of textbooks, let me offer my own personal choice of readings that I feel provide the "nuts" and "bolts" of effective management and positive thinking and can also serve as guidelines for the voting public when looking for ways to measure an applicant's leadership ability.

> (1) Kenneth Blanchard and Spencer Johnson, The One Minute Manager, William Morrow Company.
> (2) Ichak Adizes, How to Solve the Mismanagement Crisis, Adizes Institute.
> (3) Scott Alexander, Rhinoceros Success, Rhino Press.
> (4) Thomas J. Peters and Robert Waterman, Jr., In Search of Excellence, Warner Publisher.
> (5) Norman Vincent Peale, The Power of Positive Thinking, Prentice Hall.
> (6) Dale Carnegie, How to Win Friends and Influence People, Pocket Books.
> (7) Zig Ziglar, Top Performance, Fleming Revell Publishers.
> (8) Alan Loy McGinnis, Bringing Out the Best in People, Augsburg Publishing House.

Until we overhaul our training program at the graduate level, one might as well forget the notion that advanced degrees in educational administration mean qualified school administrators. Taking certain courses for certification does not mean the person is qualified to take the helm as a principal or superintendent. In too many cases, professors have little, if any, experience in school administration, let alone in public school classrooms. Instead of utilizing the clinical approach in field-based training, many paid

professionals at universities and colleges are still
wandering in and out of their ivory towers ignorant of
what is actually happening in our public schools.
Graduate schools of education have attempted to train
school administrators for years and, by and large, have
been unsuccessful primarily because the training has
been bureaucratic and meaningless.   Until graduate
schools of education choose to revise their programs
making them accountable in relation to the real world
of school administration with heavy emphasis on extended internships in the field, job fatality rates
among school administration graduates will continue to
increase.   The choice that must be made is to teach
potential school executives in the public school "operating rooms" and offer training that includes experience in rural, suburban, and urban settings including
elementary and secondary experiences regardless of
personal preference. University training programs must
train future school administrators, combining the
talents and wisdom of school practitioners and college
professors, both of whom have demonstrated competence
out on the front lines of public education.   We need
more training programs like the one currently at
Brigham Young University, College of Education.   The
basis of the program is a joint partnership between
five Utah school districts and the university.   A team
(consisting of superintendents, professors, college
dean, principals and state department personnel) are
developing a model principal training program that
will meet a variety of educational needs:

(1) Draw on the resources of the school
    districts and university,
(2) Select potential administrators who have
    demonstrated leadership qualities,
(3) Provide extended leave of absence for one
    year to each participant as a full-time
    student,
(4) Provide financial incentives for those
    enrolled in the program,
(5) Emphasize entry level skills and
    knowledge, and
(6) Provide training by competent university
    personnel as well as field-base-
    administrators working as a team.

The twelve-month training program requires field-base training outside the student's school district. An additional requirement involves training at a school level (elementary, middle, junior, or senior high school) in which the student has not worked as a teacher. School administrators in charge of the training in the field are selected based upon their performance which includes establishing a vision for their schools with school improvement plans in force, setting expectations for faculty and students, continually assessing teaching performance, and demonstrating the ability to make decisions. (Those interested may contact F. Del Wasden, Professor and Chairman of the Department of Educational Leadership, College of Education, Brigham Young University, Provo, Utah, for more information about the program.)

In a book previously mentioned, How to Solve the Mismanagement Crisis, author Ichak Adizes argues that the reason some companies (school districts) are more successful than others is because they tend to be mismanaged less. He claims that mismanagement, among other things, occurs in an organization when one management style dominates the approach one uses in supervising people with diverse needs and expectations. The importance of understanding leadership styles and how to use them effectively in a given situation is a must for every school administrator. In many graduate schools of education, a course in leadership is an elective rather than a requirement. A module of training must include this important topic on the course of study for every graduate student in school administration. In his book Adizes lists five management styles: The Lone Ranger, the Bureaucrat, the Arsonist, the Superfollower, and the Deadwood.

Let's look at each one briefly. The Lone Ranger has a compulsion to do everything himself and does not delegate. He comes early, leaves late, and does not train others because he believes he is the only one who can do things right. His associates are mere spectators who listen to him complain that there are not enough hours in the day; consequently, he never manages to plan for the future.

The Bureaucrat acts exclusively by the book and

avoids change or strong organization. His desk is
always clean. There cannot be any violation of
procedure since his priority is to follow the rules
regardless of the outcome. His subordinates are "yes
people" who do not rock the boat and do not question.

The Arsonist sets priorities on Monday and changes
them on Tuesday. He does not feel comfortable unless
things are in fluctuation or constant change, and he
loves chaos. He likes to see his subordinates constantly in a stage of crisis. The Arsonist executive
usually defeats his own purpose and winds up saying
"nothing ever gets done around here." Subordinates are
kept busy just trying to keep up with all the changes.

The Superfollower initiates ideas and plans that
will be acceptable to the largest number so he is also
known as the "Pleaser." Since he dislikes conflict, he
will dertermine which side of any conflict is strongest
and most likely to succeed and side with that part of
the issue.

The final type of management, according to Adizes,
is the Deadwood. Another example of this philosophy is
the Peter Principle. Deadwood's main goal is to survive until retirement. He smokes heavily, drinks quite
a lot, and constantly tells everyone how wonderful he
is. These managers avoid decision-making and spend a
great deal of energy avoiding trouble. This person is
under heavy stress and is at the burnout stage; consequently, an organization under him will function at the
lowest level. Subordinates are encouraged in anything
that can add to the manager's glory; but most of the
time, he is ignored by his subordinates.

Adizes' conclusion is that at times an effective
leader will be required to use any of the above styles
(excluding Deadwood). To let one style dominate one's
management practices day in and day out is simply poor
management. According to Adizes, it's knowing which
style to use in a given situation that counts.

Unfortunately, there are boards of education in
this country who have chosen to hire "Deadwood" school
administrators who are unable to make decisions when
required or who are unwilling to "rock the boat" for

fear of being fired or becoming unpopular. These people are chosen so that the board can maintain control of their schools and keep things at status quo.

In addition to the important and perilous position of being superintendent of schools, there is another management position in modern-day public school districts that is equally important and influential: the position of building principal. This administrative position has a strong influence over teacher morale, over how the parents and community perceive education in the district, and even over the board of education. It is the principal who plays a major role in determining happenings and carrying out the goals set forth by the school board. I can recall receiving approval from the board of education to initiate a program to increase student achievement. I called the principals together for an educational "sales" meeting to kick off the new project. Ideas were discussed, incentives planned, questions were "kicked" around and answered. Each principal then had the go ahead to tailor the program to fit the unique characteristics of his/her school. My goal was to motivate the principals to go back to their schools inspired to motivate their building teachers.

The program eventually became a big success, and student achievement gains went beyond all expectations. Student discipline problems were reduced drastically and student attendance increased. National attention was given to the program for outstanding accomplishments in raising student achievement scores in an urban setting with a student minority population of 55%.

Why, you may ask, was the program successful? What was done and how was it done? Who did what? The answers relating to preliminary requirements were easily identifiable: a good standardized testing program (K-12); support of the board of education, parents and local businesses; media coverage; and a vision that people understood and felt committed to. But the most important factor, by far, was the role each building principal assumed. The majority of the principals made the choice to take charge in their buildings by stating expectations for teachers, establishing a positive school climate, communicating

"Management by
encouragement
brings out the
best in people."

effectively (teachers-parents-students), and maintaining student discipline. Elementary and secondary
principals determine success or failure for any central
office launched project. So goes the principal, so
goes the school and school system.

Not every administrator in the education profession becomes the desired leader. Not every school
has a good principal. Some schools, believe it or not,
do get things done without good leadership because they
have what Dick Wynn (Team Management: Leadership by
Consensus, p. 35) from the University of Pittsburgh
calls "substitutes for leadership." One example is the
cohesive staff that is competent and supported by a
devoted parent group. But schools that advance without
principal leadership are rare. Schools may survive
with an inept principal, but they won't excel. Good
principals "take charge." They are team players, have
a vision, and become excited and publicly appreciative
when good things occur in their school buildings. They
go beyond the X or Y categories of management. Good
building administrators are **tough, tender, patient,
consistent, and flexible.** This means they have the
leadership skills to know when to be tough, consistent,
flexible and patient. No matter what great and
wonderful plans the superintendent may have, if the
dreams are to be turned into actual happenings with
success, the responsibility rests primarily on the
shoulders of each building principal within the school
district.

The principal takes a position on the "front
lines," dealing with students, teachers, parents, and
central office personnel every day. The phone rings
and rings and rings. Playground fights, students being
shot, parents upset over the discipline of their
children, gang disturbances, heating problems, school
bus breakdowns--on and on the challenges occur.
However, the principal is mainly charged with the
responsibility of making sure the children learn to
read, write, and count. A school principal cannot
succeed by sitting behind the desk each day. The
principal must know what is going on in the buildings.
As the old saying goes - No Contact; No Impact!

Several years ago, a story about a high school

principal appeared in one of the Texas newspapers. It seems that the students were not aware of what their principal looked like because they never saw him, so they decided to have a contest in which the students could draw what they thought their principal looked like. The plan was to ask someone who had seen the principal select the drawing that best resembled him. Sensing that something was going on, the school administration took legal measures to prohibit the publication of the paper. The case went to court. A hearing was held before the judge who, after listening to the evidence, gave the students permission to go ahead with their paper and the contest. The winner was announced and received a prize for his sketch. All of this publicity caused the embarrassed principal to emerge from his office.

Principals, as well as central office administrators, can choose to hide out all day behind their desks, or they can demonstrate they care and are in charge by being visible, not only in the school classrooms and halls, but at concerts, games, plays, contests, etc.

The focus so far has been directed towards the positions of superintendent of schools and school principal. This does not mean to slight or play down the importance of other administrative positions within a school system. Directors of finance, instruction, curriculum, maintenance, and special service personnel all play a major role in the total operation of any school district. It is the people in these positions that give the support and resources to superintendents and principals and collectively take charge to see to it that a well-run, efficient, and accountable educational package is provided to the students.

No position is without failure. Strong school administrators fail in many of their attempts just as weak school administrators do. However, the difference between strong school administrators and weak school administrators is that strong school administrators know where they are going, make decisions, and treat failure simply as a junction in the road. Weak school administrators avoid making decisions and permit the failures and tough times to do them in, since they fail to keep their eyes and their energies focused on their vision.

My plan for advancing as a school administrator in today's world of abounding challenges is one of choice. I submit to the reader that, by choosing to follow the principles I have listed below, the prospect will (1) be an inspiration to others, (2) be recognized as a leader, (3) improve his individual performance, and (4) probably have some new doors open with increased financial rewards.

(1) **Accept the fact you are going to make mistakes and learn from those mistakes.** Don't be afraid to admit shortcomings. Keep in mind that failure can breed success. Thomas Edison made 10,000 attempts at inventing the incandescent light bulb before he succeeded. The main thing is not to back away from a challenge. One of the characteristics that compares "poor" school administrators to "good" school administrators is that good ones don't back down when faced with a difficult situation, rather, they tackle it head on.

I have had the privilege of working with many respected school administrators who never dodged an issue. Firm and decisive, they had the respect of their faculty, community and colleagues. They weren't afraid to admit mistakes, could make decisions and knew how to effectively individualize their management styles in order to adapt to whatever the issue or issues were at the time. They saw what needed to be done and they did it. Many administrators know what needs to be done; they simply don't do it!

(2) **Have confidence in yourself and express confidence in others.** If administrators are going to administrate effectively, they must have confidence in themselves. Confidence in oneself is getting the mind in condition to think anything is possible.

I remember hearing Dan Rather stating his philosophy of handling pressure to a gathering at the time of taking over the reins from Walter Cronkite. "Don't be crushed if you fail; if you indulge yourself that way, you never put yourself in a pressure

situation again and you will never gain confidence,"
Rather stated.

Good school administrators, like good business leaders, possess confidence and know how to use it
to their advantage in solving pressure situations.
Remember that successes involve capitalizing on strong
points and working on improving weak points. A school
administrator must, at times, "rock the boat." If you
fail, regroup and try again. This will give you the
confidence to achieve.

Superintendents and school boards need to be
the leaders who spread confidence and enthusiasm
throughout the school district. A pat on the back, an
encouraging word from time to time means so much,
especially when it comes from the top. The right tonic
or dosage of positive human relations can be the best
medicine to help spur someone to greater heights and
to increase their performance. Board of education
members need to spend more of their energies publicly
supporting administration and teachers. The board and
superintendent need to keep before them the question,
"Is this decision ultimately in the best interest of
the children?" What a difference this could mean in
many school districts throughout the country.

I believe in the following words stated by
Theodore Roosevelt (<u>Motivational Quotes</u>, p. M63):

> "It is not the critic who counts, not the
> man who points out how strong men stumbled or
> where the doer of deeds could have done
> better. The credit belongs to the man who is
> actually in the arena: whose face is marred
> by dust and sweat and blood; who strives
> valiantly; who errs and comes short again and
> again; who knows the great enthusiasms, the
> great devotions, and spends himself in a
> worthy cause; who, at the best, knows in the
> end the triumph of high achievement; and who,
> at the worst, if he fails, at least fails
> while daring greatly, so that his place shall
> never be with those cold and timid souls who
> know neither victory nor defeat."

(3) **Communicate expectations: Design a playbook.**
A football coach builds his playbook around the
strengths and weaknesses of his offensive and defensive
players. Looking at each upcoming season, the coach
and his staff map their strategy in anticipation of
producing a winning season. School administrators are
no different. There is an annual need to design a
"playbook" based upon school district's priorities.
The superintendent, as well as all school administrators, must choose to prepare for each upcoming season
with specific measurable goals and objectives precisely
written to address the priorities and needs of the
school district. These priorities can then become the
basis for judging annual performance. Each administrator should have input into his own evaluation design,
and the common checklists used in many school districts
today to evaluate administrators should be recycled
into scratch pads. Certainly it is unreasonable to
expect teachers to accept revised and newly-adopted
evaluation programs when administrators are still using
forms and procedures that lack accountability and are
not in tune with modern-day management practices that
foster improved performance.

Any good leader worth his salt knows what is
going on, where he wants to go, and how to get there.
Successful school administrators, like successful business leaders, have a vision, possess enthusiasm, and
set goals. Therefore, if a leader wants to make things
happen in a school district, to upgrade the curriculum,
to improve student achievement, or to expand effective
community relations, he needs to design a playbook and
communicate effectively exactly what the expectations
and goals are that have been decided upon.

Keep in mind each school building has unique
characteristics different from other schools within the
same district. Each principal, for example, has unique
professional strengths and weaknesses. A general
checklist form of evaluation ignores individual personnel differences. Choosing to use a well-designed
MBO (Management by Objectives) playbook based on
priorities and needs combined with an effective format
will make all leaders at the school and district levels
accountable and will increase the chances of having a
winning season.

"Holding people
accountable
breeds
support."

(4) **Dress for success.** This fourth criteria is a must if one deals directly with the public. Anyone who has conducted interview sessions can almost predict how the interview will go by the way the candidate is dressed. It is worth the investment for the interviewee to purchase tailored, neat, appropriate clothing. Students gain respect for teachers and administrators who, as dress expert John T. Malloy states, "Dress for Success." First impressions mean a lot, especially when dealing with the public or speaking before a group. It sends a visual message that you care. Psychologically, it can give you more authority. "Wardrobe engineering," says Malloy modestly, "is just putting together elements of psychology, fashion, sociology and art" (Marling, p. 15). Educational administrators can take a lesson on dress from the people at General Motors, International Business Machine and Standard Oil. They dress for success. In many organizations men and women cannot leave their desks without putting on their suit jackets.

Although a school district cannot legally enforce dress codes for teachers, much can be done to improve faculty appearances throughout a school building and district by having administrative personnel set the example. Good dress can become contagious, especially if the administrators set the example and reinforce teachers who make an effort. There have been studies done on the effects of dress upon the behavior of students. Such research endeavors offer far more sense and practicality in addressing discipline problems and behavior patterns in our schools than some of the dissertation work coming out of the graduate schools of education. In my graduate courses in educational administration that I teach at Clemson University, the word is out that if a student wants to get off to the right start in Fuhr's class, dress professionally. Recently I was told the University Board of Trustees were meeting in Room 208, Tillman Hall, which is where most of the classes meet in the College of Education. To my surprise, it turned out that the "Board of Trustees" were my students dressed with coats, ties, and tailored suits and dresses. When I teach, I dress appropriately and professionally, and I expect my students to do the same. Some professors and administrators "model" sloppy dress and create a nonprofessional atmosphere when they do so. In elementary and secondary schools, sloppy dress on the part of the faculty invariably suggests to the public that so are their classrooms and their performance.

(5) **Give it all you have.** When one in a leadership position desires to change or accomplish something in any organization, he has three distinct classifications of people to deal with. First, there are those within the organization who are receptive to change. Next, there are those who don't really understand the reason for change, but could be swayed. Finally, you have those who simply reject all thoughts of change and feel comfortable with a "status quo" situation. The present day school administrator is challenged to enlist the support from those who understand the need for improvement who in turn will urge the "fence riders" to get off the fence and join the team.

The theme of the movie <u>Chariots of Fire</u> was "Give me an arrow of desire and set my chariot on fire." How we need to light a fire of burning desire in public education! Public education needs administrators who can be decisive and make the changes necessary to improve education in our country, administrators who become alive inside themselves and "rev" up their determination, administrators who have enough enthusiasm that it infuses everything and everyone with whom they come in contact.

The preceding five principles - (1) Accept the fact you will make mistakes and learn from those mistakes, (2) Have confidence in yourself, (3) Communicate expectations, (4) Dress for success, and (5) Give it all you have - are the pillars upon which the foundation for success begins to be built in today's world of public school administration. We do have many well managed schools in this country! There is a sincere and dedicated effort to follow policy and maintain existing structures so that education can take place. But what is lacking in many of our public schools is bold, decisive, courageous leadership. Such leadership means being willing to go out on a tree limb when you hear the buzz saw going off behind you! It means taking a stand against radical special self-interest groups who desire to gain control of the school building or district and, subsequently, destroy the roots of quality education. It means addressing issues when they occur and making decisions that will be unpopular but in the long run will be in the best interest of the students and school district.

Of course, as in any corporate structure, we have some school administrators who simply are not able to administrate effectively because they have not been given the support and the freedom to move ahead. Either the board of education or central office administration (or both) has chosen to throw up road blocks to hinder advancement. Administrators are hired to administrate effectively, not to be "yes" people. Even more important is the fact that, with the complexity of today's public school operations, no one person or group can do the job and do it well. It takes administrative leadership, community support, and teamwork and persistence in a school district in order to have good things happening for children. Accountable school administration mandates professionals to travel in the same direction toward stated goals.

There are many school principals who demonstrate what effective school administration is all about.

Carmen Guappone, now retired, was principal of German Central Elementary School, McClellandtown, Pennsylvania. He completed his doctoral work at the University of Pittsburgh under the expert direction of Brad Seager, one of the pioneers in clinical supervision. McClellandtown had high crime rates, illiteracy, and unemployment. Many of its citizens were on welfare because of high layoffs within the steel industry. Guappone knew what had to be done as leader and went about doing it. Once a dropout himself, he took charge by making school a place where <u>all</u> students would experience potential success regardless of test scores. Programs were developed for the gifted with emphasis on creative writing and problem solving. In addition, Guappone was able to secure TV equipment so that the students could tape their performance in the arts. The school put on the production <u>Rich Man, Poor Man</u>, and some 400 students tried out for various parts. Without his leadership, many of these young students would never have had the opportunity for such an experience.

Carmen Guappone took charge and made things happen in his school.

"You have to roll up your sleeves and work that much harder," states another effective principal, Jimmie Warren, at James Monroe High School in the Bronx. He was referring to the "insurmountable problems" he faces every day. He has faced problems before as principal of four other troubled schools in New York City, and he has conquered overwhelming odds with his positive affirming approach to the students and faculty. "You can't intimidate people into learning. You can't use a baseball bat and say, 'Hey you: Learn.' You have to serve as a positive role model." He initiated the adopt-a-student program. Faculty members "adopted" students whom they visited, encouraged, tutored and/or invited to their homes. The school had active parent and community support and 80% of the graduates now go on to continue their education. Warren sees all the students as super achievers having great potential. "All they need is proper encouragement," Warren states (Ryan, pp. 18-21).

One of the best ways to build credibility into school district operations is to monitor and evaluate happenings and report findings. Some administrators think they can fool "John Q. Public" by not coming forth with results on school achievement. They are afraid of repercussions. What better way to gain support than to announce findings, show strengths as well as weaknesses, and then design a plan of action to sustain strengths and improve the weak areas.

Phil Musgrave, principal of Strom Thurmond High School (a school located in the heart of the peach country), Johnston, South Carolina, is a highly respected leader to students, faculty, and community people. Musgrave spends his entire day away from his office, returning after school hours to complete necessary paperwork and handle correspondence. Phil Musgrave is a master doing what some writers of education call "one minute mingling." He is in and out of every teacher's classroom on a daily basis making decisions, praising, asking questions, and privately reprimanding students (and teachers), if necessary. The visibility of this school administrator and his

openness to faculty and students followed by decisive
leadership has been the backbone for the success of a
school which serves a blue collar semi-rural community.
During the last several years, daily student attendance
has risen to 96.4% and daily teacher attendance to
96.0%. Strom Thurmond High School has been the reci-
pient of South Carolina's Incentive Award for the past
several years. This award includes additional financial support based on instructional achievement gains.
The majority of graduates go on to four-year college
programs. Strom Thurmond High has had its share of
merit scholarship finalists, and the math and history
teams have won state championships.

George McKenna, subject of a national television
movie several years ago entitled The George McKenna
Story, was principal at the George Washington Preparatory High School in Los Angeles. He turned a drug-
ridden school into a respected one by requiring quality
teaching (those teachers who failed to produce were not
rehired) and by requiring proper student conduct (those
students who refused to follow policy were expelled or
suspended). But, the big factor that made McKenna
successful as an inner city high school principal was
his caring for his students. McKenna was stern, firm
and humble. George McKenna had a vision for George
Washington Preparatory High School and he stuck to it.
He fought the odds and won. Following the airing of
the movie he stated, "Television has a tendency to
ascribe the responsibilities for a negative school
sometimes to the children and to gangs who, in fact,
are victims themselves of lack of leadership and
guidance on the part of professionals."

The key ingredient relating to these school
administrators - and all successful, effective administrators - is that they are leaders, eager to assume
responsibility and make decisions. They are take-
charge people who choose to have a game plan based on
priorities and needs of the school building and community. These administrators communicate expectations
and get results. They use a variety of management
styles in addressing challenges. They are action
people with a vision and mold a team to help reach that
vision.

"Students expect and
desire discipline
in their schools."

There are school administrators who are afraid to tackle problems. They are the "status quo's" and "fence riders" mentioned earlier. A good example of where the action school administrators are distinguished from the "non-action" fence rider types is over the issue of dropouts. Presently (1989), one out of four students drops out of school before the twelfth grade, amounting to 3,600 youngsters per day according to Education Secretary Lauro Cavazos (AASA, Leadership News, p. 1). It takes courage for school administrators to stand up to parents and say, "Look, our job is to educate children while in school. We will do all we can to make your child learn to read, write, and count. But it's your job to see that they come to school." Some parents drop their children off at kindergarten, and the next time we see them is at graduation. We must stop blaming our schools for causing children to drop out of school. "Fence rider" administrators will respond to concerned parents by saying (1) there will be a district-wide blue ribbon committee formed to study the situation, (2) we are "working" on the problem, or (3) additional funds are being requested to keep students from dropping out. Money is not a cure in the prevention of students dropping out of school. Committee meetings can serve as a stalling technique, and responding with "we are working on the problem," soon loses its appeal. Effective school administrators reduce dropout figures by assessing their problems (cause), reviewing programs (analysis), and then implementing steps (action) to address the problem. The cure is immediate action, not prolonged delay.

For too long, school districts have played defensive ball in tackling controversial issues. Parents must be told that schools are not miracle production factories. All the ills of society cannot be laid at the doorstep of public education. Parents need to hear the message that they have a major responsibility in the rearing of their children, not the public schools.

The choice must be made to improve our public schools, starting at the top with qualified members on the board of education coupled with school administrators who carry out the policies of the school system (management), on one hand, and to use courageous, decisive and creative techniques (leadership) on the other.

We can't afford to have our public education system in
this country go "bankrupt." Boards of education must
continually strive to rid themselves of political connections and maneuvering and to concentrate more on
providing and supporting policies that directly and
indirectly support quality education. One of the most
important choices that the public must make is to support a solid management team led by a superintendent of
schools. Once the team is in place, school administrators cannot be interferred with as they go about
carrying out the policies of the school district, and
they equally must have support and extended job security. It is my belief that school superintendents should
be chosen by qualified people representing the educational, business and private sectors along with the
school board. Popular vote usually insures the perpet-
uation of the "good ole boy."

Superintendents, in turn, must hold principals
accountable for student achievement, teacher evaluation, discipline, community relations, and upkeep of
buildings, while principals must hold teachers accountable for student performance, discipline, and their own
professionalism. Principals must address poor teaching
in their schools, provide remediation; and if progress
fails, they must then take the initiative to recommend
dismissal. Superintendents must follow the same path
in evaluating their administrators. There are over
100,000 school administrators (compared with more than
two million teachers) who need to take charge and
reveal to teachers that they know what is going on.
Administrators at all levels must choose to be "action
people," who are bold enough to venture into unknown
waters if necessary to make good things happen.

Can administrators administrate? The term administrate should include leadership as well as managing;
and in my opinion, the majority of public school administrators in this country are effective leaders as well
as managers. For example, if a top level CEO of a
Fortune 500 company were to walk into your school
district to assess leadership and management practices,
what would you guess the findings would be? Would he
praise the school district for its fine efforts in
running an efficient organization? Would your school
administrators demonstrate leadership? Could the CEO

identify a management team vision that had been planned and communicated to the staff and public? Would the visiting CEO notice that morale, loyalty and dedication is a visible trademark of the entire staff? Or, instead, would the CEO say, "If my company ran things the way you are doing it here in the school district, I can assure you we would have been closed down years ago!"

As noted earlier, our public schools in the United States are no doubt the best managed schools in the world. Daily routines are followed, budgets are planned, policies are adhered to in most cases, and the job is done according to a set of guidelines. What separates schools that work from apathetic, unmotivated schools is leadership. Leadership involves stimulating change for progress. Leadership means creating a climate within an organization where people are motivated and willing to produce without having to be told. Leaders are those individuals who have an understanding of leadership styles and know how to use them effectively. They learn from their mistakes, have confidence in themselves and express confidence in others, communicate expectations, dress for success, and give it all they have. School districts must make the choice to hire and keep administrators in today's schools that possess these basic principles. Today's school administrator holds the key that unlocks the door of success for future generations.

This chapter has set forth information about qualifications and qualities that administrators should have. Administrators who read this chapter may ask themselves if they are fulfilling these expectations. The public can ask themselves the same question regarding their choice of administrators.

Public education will improve when daring, bold, and courageous school administrators at the helm of our schools and school districts will proudly lead our public education system into the 21st century.

Chapter 3

Can Teachers Teach?

*"A child is a person who is going to carry
on what you have started. He is going to
sit where you are sitting, and, when you
are gone, attend to those things which you
think are important. You may adopt all the
policies you please, but how they will be
carried out depends on him. He will assume
control of your cities, states, and nations.
He is going to move in and take over your
churches, schools, universities and
corporations. All your books are going
to be judged by him. The fate of humanity
is in his hands."*

--Abraham Lincoln

What a potentially dynamic force we have attending
our schools for approximately 180 days each school
year! What happens to this dynamic force of students
as they sit in classrooms? Are they learning what they
need to know, or are they simply scraping by, year
after year, until they can "get out?" Are they
inspired, motivated, challenged, and inbred with a
desire to learn through the efforts of devoted
teachers?

John T. Goodlad, author of "A Place Called
School," in an interview for Education Week commented
on the differences in our schools and in our classrooms. Goodlad and his colleagues at U.C.L.A. revealed
clearly that the differences in schools and classrooms
have more to do with human relationships than anything
else. One researcher stated:

> reject teachers who have favorites.
> They reject teachers who use
> sarcasm. They like teachers who
> help them when they're in trouble;
> they like teachers who are enthusi-
> astic; they like teachers who seem
> to like their work. These are the
> things that differentiate among our
> schools. The methods of teaching
> don't; the curriculum doesn't.

Goodlad said, "You can bring the love of learning into the classroom enthusiastically and still have a good solid math program and a good solid English program, with a lot of varied approaches."

There is no question that what occurs in a class-room is at the sole discretion of the teacher. It's the teacher that counts. You can have a well-designed curriculum, with accompanying learning materials, supported by a comprehensive testing program to measure student learning, and a motivating family atmosphere, but this will not inspire students to learn. The key to fostering learning in any school is the principal and the teacher, for it is these two positions that will determine how much Johnny, Susie, Robbie, and Katie will or will not learn.

I can never forget my first teaching experience. After spending six years in retail management work with the Goodyear Tire and Rubber Company, I left the industrial world and returned to my native state, West Virginia, in 1963. There I enrolled as a graduate student at West Virginia University. My goal was to be a teacher. Although I appreciated the corporate world, I had always been fascinated with the idea of teaching.

With enough money saved for tuition and moving, my family and I left St. Mary's, Ohio, for Morgantown in January, 1963. My enthusiasm for the classroom sky-rocketed when I began teaching junior and senior high students in a Sunday School class at the First Chris-tian Church in Morgantown. It is my contention that if you can hold the interest and attention of ten to twelve youths each Sunday, your chances of succeeding as a classroom teacher are good. As attendance in-

about that dedicated faculty and the students
m I had the pleasure of knowing. I have since
two of my former students in that Room 6 Ameri-
ory class gave their lives in Vietnam. That is
son when I later became superintendent of
I dedicated myself to the notion that I would
orsake the students. So many of my former
have given me so much in the way of intangible
that I will always cherish the memories.

things are changing. National Education
ion figures in 1981 revealed that the average
f teacher services has dropped from 20 years to
in the past two decades (Educators Newsletter,
Combined with the fact that teachers are under-
appears the old "dedication is the reason I
otion is wearing thin.

is a fact that education reform in the United
will fail as the "least academically able"
teachers unless something is done to raise the
on's standards, status and pay. According to a
poration report in a study entitled, Beyond the
on Reports: The Coming Crisis in Education,
he search for excellence as it is being con-
in most states will not solve the problem. The
warned that the nation faces severe teacher
es unless steps are taken to professionalize
. The report recommended that teacher salaries
$20,000 annually and reach $50,000.

n teachers teach? Yes, there are many that
o teach and are teaching effectively. In fact,
be the last hope in public education. If more
e of the "good ones" choose to leave, then
education is on the brink of disaster. The
is what is being done to get rid of the dead-
d what is being done to support and encourage
essful teachers?

achers don't always demand smaller classes or
salaries. The Virginia Journal of Education
eachers what would most help them become better
? Heading the list was support from parents,
munity and the school administration. Smaller
ize was seventh, after higher salaries, better

creased in that Sunday School class, my eagerness to
start teaching in a public school grew. I conducted
the Sunday class on the same basis as a qualified secondary teacher would teach American history, English,
or math. Incentives to bolster attendance were used,
student discipline was maintained, variation in teaching methods were incorporated; and much preparation
went into each lesson. Most important, I cared for
every young person who attended. The initial success
that I was experiencing in this Sunday school class
eventually served to inspire me to greater heights in
teaching as well as administration.

The opportunity to join the ranks as a public
school teacher came during my second year of graduate
work at the university. I was offered a position to
teach social studies (American History - Problems of
Democracy) at the eleventh and twelfth grades at
University Laboratory High School, which I eagerly
accepted at an annual salary of $3000! The school was
listed as a laboratory school and was directed and
operated by the graduate school of education at the
university. The majority of students came from middle
to low income families.

As a roving teacher, I was assigned five different
classrooms a day. That never bothered me, because when
I entered each classroom I became even more excited
about teaching. One of my favorite groups was an
eleventh grade American history class. Every day as I
walked down the hall to Room 6, bottom floor, right
under the office of the principal, I anticipated the
greetings I would receive upon opening the door. I had
been told to keep tight reins on this group because if
you "gave them an inch, they would take a mile."
Students were grouped into classes based on achievement
scores. This particular class in Room 6 was listed as
"low ability." I have always been opposed to using
test scores to predetermine how much a student can
learn. Coming into the class each day, I can still
remember so clearly their welcoming words, "Hey, Mr.
Fuhr, how are you doing today?", "What are we going to
do today, Mr. Fuhr?", "It's too hot to study, Mr. Fuhr;
let's go outside and take a walk." Like my Sunday
School class, I felt all along that if I could motivate
these students to learn I could probably achieve un-

"Teacher attitude is more important than teacher knowledge."

limited heights in all future teaching

I had respect for them, and they
me. They knew when I meant busines
accordingly. Never once did I have a
lem or cause myself to be backed in
would cause the students to lose res
some of them "out of jams" during scho
doing so, they were quite appreciati
only read on the third and fourth gr
ever that means), but what a class
varied my teaching techniques, us
materials, put emphasis on oral read
project and independent study time for
current events; and we learned togeth
they, maybe more so in my case. I s
names of most of the students. Teac
volunteered to chaperone the dances an
the football and basketball games.
that most teachers don't "fail" in te
lack of knowledge but because of ineff
in their teaching and an unwillingnes
with their school and its students.

There were no special self-intere
ing to change this or that. There
pending contract disputes. There wer
meetings to attend. Mr. Nine, the
school, and Dr. Delmas Miller, direct
were the administrators and did an ex
faculty was superb, dedicated, and hi
Graduates of the school went on to th
emy, West Point, and the Naval Acade
liberal arts colleges and did quite
into the labor market and were produc

Now as I reflect back, I wonder
the students I taught at University
twenty years ago. I left after one
teaching position in Middletown, Ma
because of a substantial salary
annually. Later, my travels took
Virginia at Weir High School in Wei
tinued my enthusiasm for teaching.
school in Morgantown is no longer in
ran short, and the university decide

won
with
lear
can
one
scho
neve
stud
rewa

Asso
leng
14 y
p. 3
paid
teac

Stat
becon
profe
Rand
Commi
1988,
ducte
repo
short
teach
start

choos
they
and m
publi
quest
wood,
the s

highe
asked
teache
the c
class

and more frequent in-service training, more aides and clerical assistance. Last was unlimited supplies and materials.

In the last chapter, we mentioned the indecisiveness on the part of school administrators and school boards to deal with the problem of poor teaching in our schools. Although incompetent teachers present a major problem in public education, they are seldom fired because administrators and school boards are wary of court fights that can cost upwards of $100,000.00 per case. It is my opinion that in every school building in this country, 15% of the total teaching personnel are incompetent. You multiply this percentage by the total number of teachers in a school system or by the total number of teachers in this country (2.3 million) and you have a staggering figure of 345,000 incompetent teachers in our elementary and secondary classrooms throughout the country.

A study financed by the National Institute of Education urged schools to develop written review systems, meeting specified criteria to safely and effectively weed out ineffective teachers. Conducted by the Institute for Research on Educational Finance and Governance and the Clearinghouse on Educational Management, the study examined one of the most controversial topics in education today: what to do with teachers who can't teach. The study found that only about half the nations 16,000 school districts now have established evaluation programs, and many are so inadequate they would be unable to stand up in court (Education U.S.A., p. 318).

In 1977 a poll of members of the American Association of School Administrators found respondents estimating that from five to fifteen percent of their teachers are "unsatisfactory performers." "Yet dismissals are extremely rare," the study reported, noting a review of two publications which track teacher employment court cases and found only eighty-six cases of tenured teachers being fired between 1939 and 1982 (Beacon News, p. 13). It is undermining to teachers who effectively do their jobs to have incompetent teachers, protected by tenure, earning as much and sometimes more income. Good teachers wish "the management" would remove the ineffective teachers.

There will no doubt continue to be increasing demands for more discipline, more homework, longer school days, a longer school year and harder courses in valiant hope that this will improve test scores. These changes will not improve and upgrade the teaching profession. Pounding the pavement, boycotts, blue flu, and more reform packages will not increase teacher performance. In 1987, seventeen states required prospective teachers to take the NTE (National Teacher Exam) while some seventeen other states administered a similar exam developed for them by outside agencies. Three states (Arkansas, Texas, Georgia) required veteran teachers to pass a recertification exam. The exams cover subject matter knowledge as well as basic skills (generic) (Madaus and Pullin, p. 31). As important as these tests are, do they guarantee good teaching? Does the mastery of subject knowledge and basic skill understanding mean that a person is qualified to teach? The clinical training programs offered by many higher education training institutions that are supposed to prepare student teachers for teaching positions in our public schools are extremely weak and out of touch with reality. Many future teachers are not trained to handle the diverse population of students found in school districts.

There are approximately 1500 teacher training institutions in the United States today. A vast majority of these teacher preparation institutions offer a limited six- to twelve-week student teaching program, usually taken in a student's senior year. With a satisfactory student teaching experience (grade of C is acceptable) and the passing of state certified courses plus an acceptable score on the NTE, a student is granted a certificate to teach. Although a test is given in most states to determine if the student knows the subject he or she is about to teach, little emphasis has been directed towards finding out if the student can actually teach. Mastery of the art of teaching cannot be determined by taking a block of courses that are required for certification, being involved in a limited student teaching experience, and taking an exam that determines knowledge of subject and the ability to use basic generic skills that are used in teaching. Such a program only goes half way. The other half is attempting to determine if the student can teach. Present-day teacher competency tests do not address vital requirements of good teaching such as initiative, enthusiasm, organization, and caring.

To prepare future teachers, institutions of higher learning must begin knocking down the barriers that presently exist between the training institutions and school districts. This requires developing a teacher training team that includes capable school administrators, capable teachers, capable professors working side by side in developing a curriculum that should include the following experiences under a five-year program.

1. A two-year internship (freshman, sophomore) program which includes classroom observations, attending seminars, serving as a teacher aide, being assigned reading assignments and a basic grasp of the psychology of achievement principles. At the completion of the second year, students would be assessed and counseled regarding their continuation in the program.

2. A program of study which, in addition to subject area requirements, includes courses in test and measurement (test construction), verbal/non-verbal communications, individualized instruction, psychology of learning, curriculum development, and instructional media development (construction of learning activities).

3. A one-year clinical teaching experience which emphasizes the use of various teaching strategies, coping with student needs, evaluation of instructional programs, working and communicating effectively with parents and local community organizations and developing self-evaluation techniques.

4. At the completion of the fifth year, all students would be required to pass an oral and written examination to assess their competencies in teaching and knowledge of

subject matter.

5.   Upon satisfactory completion of the assess-
      ment program, a student would be granted a
      license to teach at the elementary or
      secondary level.

It is reasonable to expect and require a full year
of clinical teaching in rural, suburban, and urban
classroom settings under the watchful eye of a
respected mentor and supervisor before any prospective
teacher is granted a license to teach in our public
schools. All facets of teaching skills would be used
and monitored and heavy use would be made of video
feedback.   The training would take place in the
"operating rooms" of public education, the local school
district.

Recently three midwestern cities - Gary, Hammond,
and East Chicago, Indiana - chose to train their own
teachers on the job. Fed up with not being able to
attract or hire competent urban teachers from the
university, the administrative leadership of these
three school districts got their heads together and
worked out a training program with Indiana University
Northwest. The choice to train teachers "on site"
using successful veteran teachers skilled in urban
teaching created a revolutionary shift in the training
of teachers from the university to the urban schools.
One school site was designated in each of the three
districts staffed with joint school-university faculty
that would train and recommend teachers for certification. The training program required up to two years
of supervised on-the-job teaching before certification
was granted.

The choice made by the superintendents of these
three urban school districts to do something about the
quality of teaching candidates graduating from the
university reveals what can be done when a commitment
is made to turn a vision into reality. In this case,
designing a school-based training program for future
urban teachers that will prepare them to teach
effectively in an urban school environment is a
tremendous idea. It takes the training of teachers out
of the "make believe" university classrooms and puts it

right smack into the real world of public education. The majority of our educational training programs must choose to follow suit by hiring professionals who are skilled masters in the field of administration and teaching based on their strong background in public school administration and teaching.

Once professionally trained, we must provide these teachers with improved conditions for teaching, starting in each school district's own backyard. School boards often make a mistake by first trying to approach state and federal agencies for more money. A more effective choice would entail mobilizing local talents such as sending out special RSVP invitations to community leaders, Chamber of Commerce representatives, personnel managers of local plants, beauticians, bankers, clergy, and others to tour the school district. An orientation session should be offered by the central office staff prior to school visitations. As these key people get into classrooms and talk to teachers, powerful support groups have the opportunity to form. Such a procedure offers key influential people in a school district a chance to see the product (quality education) they are being asked to invest in (higher taxes referendum, etc.) before they buy it.

Once this group gets behind and supports the education movement, efforts can continue through the PTA, PTO, and staff. The goal is to effectively sell the product to the entire community. It is foolish to think that individual school administrators led by the superintendent can do the job by themselves. The task requires everyone's support. It is heartening to teachers to see their superintendent and school board members involved in the schools they serve; whether their involvement includes a word of appreciation or active participation in some function of the school. It is equally important to have community leaders who use public relations, media, and word of mouth to effectively stress the needs and positive happenings in the school.

According to an article in the Greenville News, "A Teaching Revolution," the Rochester, New York, school system is a prime example where everyone has gotten into the act of supporting education. The Urban League

"Parents are not
always sending
schools their
best products."

of Rochester, Center for Educational Development (non-profit foundation), university, business, government, union and the local media chose to muster their forces together to focus the community of Rochester on (1) why it was important to have good public education and (2) what it would take to achieve the results. The outcome has been the formulation of a vision. The vision of the Rochester Public Schools states all children can learn and the obligation of the schools is to become responsible to all children so they can learn with the incorporation of new instructional programs. Some of Rochester's schools currently stand among the best in the country.

Even though things are happening in states to address the critical issues in public education, more needs to be done to upgrade teaching. Higher salaries alone will not be a cure-all for the current ills of public education. However, a three-way drive to acquire higher salaries, attain better supervision and evaluation of teachers, and seek total community backing by supporting teachers and school activities will serve to bolster public educators in our country.

Teachers and administrators can't do everything that needs to be done in the education of children. The main responsibility of the school is to teach children in order to prepare them for a future in society. That is the sole mission of a school. Other responsibilities relating to the upbringing of a child rests with the home. However, what has happened is that our schools have had forced on them the responsibilities that society does not want to handle. With both parents working, single parent homes, and the breakdown of communication within the family, a heavy burden has been placed on our public schools in this country. The schools are expected to take over the parents' role in raising their children, and that is not the job of public schools. There is a lack of stability in the home which has a direct bearing upon how the child acts when he comes to school. In describing the kind of students presently entering our schools, one professional educator recently commented, "parents aren't sending us their best." The outcome is that elementary and secondary classroom teachers are faced with classroom disruptions, and many are not prepared to handle them. Student attacks on teachers, gangs, custody cases, and truancy reflect the fallout from our changing society and, consequently, filter into the public school classrooms throughout the United States.

Teachers become frustrated, and, therefore, want more job security and support from parents as well as administrators. This situation is repeated time after time in public education today. Every student that comes knocking on the door of any public school in this country must be admitted, providing legal custody is in order. It is not surprising to find some schools in the country having a student turnover rate between September and mid-January as high as 30-40 percent. That means that almost half of the students that enrolled in September are no longer in school come January. It is not difficult to see why an increasing number of teachers are becoming frustrated and downhearted. This trend must change.

If I were to ask you to name three people who had influence upon your life, I dare say one would be a teacher. Your favorite teacher was no doubt one that was fair to students, consistent in administering discipline, had the respect of the total class, and, most important, he cared about you as a human being. I remember my favorite. His name was E. E. Roberts, a journalism and public relations professor at Bethany College, a small liberal arts school located in the hills of West Virginia where I did my undergraduate work. "Prof," as we called him, never gave a formal test or exam as is routinely done in grades K - graduate school. He was an enormous man, not in physical stature but in vision and inspiration. There was little, if any, student absenteeism because each student knew that his thoughts and ideas would be accepted with understanding and enthusiasm. He was always accessible despite many demands upon his time. He had the ability to inspire students to go beyond their expectations. "Prof" made learning come alive! Having been a professor at the college since 1928, he knew the "ins" and "outs" of college students. He would never downgrade his students. "Prof" assigned individuals thought-provoking topics in order to inspire individual initiative. He keenly observed and encouraged students growing in wisdom and maturity. He wanted the best for each and every one. The impression that "Prof" Roberts left upon me is still very vivid even today. His manners and professionalism, his caring demeanor, his knowledge of subject were attributes that have had a lasting effect on me. I teach graduate level courses in educational administration within the College of Education at Clemson University. Students have continually evaluated my teaching with high marks and gratitude. As I am writing this section, I received a call from a father (retired) whose daughter is presently in one of my classes. He stated, "Dr. Fuhr, I just wanted to call you to let you know how much my daughter appreciates your class." (His daughter is a teacher.) "She came home last night excited, motivated and praising you to the high heavens. So when she called me to tell me about your class, I wanted to call you and let you know how much we as parents, appreciate hearing this good news from our daughter." I thanked the gentleman for taking time to call me which was indeed a very thoughtful gesture. My teaching success since leaving the field of public school administration some four years ago is certainly due in part to the twenty-three years I spent on the "front lines." There is no substitute, believe me, for actual job experience. But I also feel that my success in the classroom originates from my desire to be not just a good teacher, but a superb one. I recall the inspiration I received each time I entered "Prof" Roberts class. He made his words come alive. As students enter my classes, I want them to leave inspired, excited and knowledgeable. I remind them, "You paid money to enroll in my class; therefore, it is my duty to make your investment pay off with interest by structuring an accountable, stimulating semester of work." I assure them that they will complete the course with greater insight and understanding than when they entered, and such an outcome is worth more than the cost of the course.

Incidentally, my method of teaching works in reverse when compared to other methods where the majority of teaching evolves around notetaking, reading, homework, memorizing and then testing. I provide the students with the questions at the beginning of the semester, then guide them towards the answers. Those

who have read the popular <u>One Minute Manager</u> by Kenneth
Blanchard and Spencer Johnson recall their emphasis on
developing well-defined goals as a key for achievement.
Likewise, I determine the most important things that I
want to teach and have the students learn. Next, I
convert these topics into goals. Everyone knows what
the goals are. They are visible, written down, and
obtainable. Thus, providing the students up front with
the questions (goals transformed into questions) that
will be forthcoming on an upcoming exam excites and
motivates them to want to achieve. I do not lay down
roadblocks or plan sneak attacks that would interfere
with the learning. My approach to teaching is based
upon a common understanding of achievement: We all
like to work for or be taught by someone who (1) outlines specifically where we are going (goals), (2)
provides support and assistance (praise) along the way,
and (3) gives feedback (evaluation) on how we are
doing. I have observed that in addition to the positive excitement and motivation that each student
demonstrates, there is individual competition among
themselves to want to achieve as the course proceeds.
Providing the students with the test questions and then
joining them and guiding them in using the proper tools
to come up with the answers is a revolutionary method
of teaching for many. The choice to incorporate this
so-called reverse method of teaching originated from my
belief that many education textbooks of and by themselves do not relate to the everyday happenings in the
field. They are merely resource information banks and
for the most part lack the "nuts and bolts" from which
to build a solid training program. Education is a
people's business, and we need course structures that
deal with the techniques and strategies of how to
effectively work with people and students. Corporate
executives who have been successful in the business
world, for example, have been those individuals who
have cared about others and have created a working
environment where people strive to reach their full
potential.

The teacher you recalled as among those individuals who had a strong influence upon your life was
more than just an individual who did something unique
or helped you out of a mess or two. He was actually a
"miracle worker." Such teachers were people that

somehow were extraordinary and, besides caring for us and others, were powerful thinkers. When we look back, how well we remember the great challengers, most of whom were teachers, who did so much for us that we can never forget them. They created in us a desire to learn. Believe me, we need more "favorites" like yours and mine in today's public classrooms. They knew the "ins" and "outs" of the art of teaching and could adjust their teaching to meet the needs of the students.

There are still many excellent teachers around, all the way from the elementary grades up to and including the ranks of the colleges and universities. But the supply is dwindling. The choice must be made to change things if the quality of teaching is to be maintained in our schools throughout the country. The choice must be made to provide financial and emotional support for our public school teachers. Such support will give confidence and encouragement to those teachers who give so much of themselves day in and day out. We all like to be praised and rewarded for a job well done; and by doing so, our attitudes can change immediately from negative to positive.

Teaching 180 days before a present-day elementary or secondary classroom of students is among the most challenging responsibilities one can every hope to face in a lifetime. I have suggested that our high schools contain no more than 500 students with a class size per teacher in the low twenties. The same number applies to elementary, middle, and junior high schools. As mentioned in Chapter 1, states are now addressing class size by mandating maximum class sizes in the basic subjects. However, the figures must come down even more through increased financial support.

In line with providing support to teachers, as a former superintendent of schools, I would always attempt to show the teaching staff that their efforts were appreciated. One thing that I did was to ask principals to send me the names of three or more teachers (number would depend on the size of the school) they would like to have me visit - "veterans" or "rookies," it didn't make any difference. As the names came in, my secretary would schedule the date of

my upcoming visit. At the same time, I would ask the
teachers for their "game plan" for the day. In other
words, I wanted to see in advance their teaching goals
and objectives. I also made it very clear that I
wanted them to give me something to do. My visit was
not to be an evaluation. The intent was to keep me
abreast of classroom happenings and staff needs.   I
refused to sit in back of the classroom and take notes
on what was good or bad; that's the principal's job. I
wanted to see the students' reaction to the teacher,
have a chance to work with students, and finally get a
chance to talk informally with the teacher. After my
visit I would send the teacher a letter thanking him
for the visit. My endeavors found me running the gamut
from finger-painting with kindergarten youngsters to
teaching a unit on Civil War history to eleventh grade
students. I enjoyed the experiences immensely and felt
it brought the superintendent's office closer to classroom happenings. One day found me at an elementary
school helping the students make stone soup. Mrs.
Johnson, a veteran 4th grade teacher, and a good one,
had the students studying a unit on the Pilgrims.
After my visit she sent me the following letter and
also one from a student named Mary B.

                                   January 6, 1981

Dear Dr. Fuhr,

     Thank you for visiting our
classroom. All of us enjoyed your being
there and your excellent assistance.

     The next day I asked the children to
write about what they had enjoyed most
about Stone Soup Day. Almost every
child mentioned your being there. I
want you to know how much good will you
are extending to students and teachers.

     We would love to have you visit
again. You don't have to make an
appointment.

                         Sincerely,

                                    Florence Johnson
                                    Fourth Grade - Brady

P.S. I am not applying for a position
as a cook!

                        December 17, 1980

     I liked best of all when we were
with Dr. Fuhr cutting the cabbage. I
like him alot because he was very nice
and I just liked him. I liked too when
we were cooking the Stone Soup. I also
liked eating it. That was the best part
of it all. Except meeting Dr. Fuhr.

                        Mary B.

     Besides higher salaries and extended fringe
benefit packages, teachers also want to be recognized
from time to time. Teachers appreciate seeing central
office personnel in their school buildings. It conveys
the message that someone cares, especially when the
superintendent takes the time for a visit. Such practices also tend to reduce the adversary relationship
between the teaching staff and the administration found
in too many school districts. What this practice
requires is a change in agenda. It requires putting
personal things to do after school hours or on the
evening schedule and putting employees interests and
input first during the regular school hours. There is
no question that the sacrifice of having to put the
paper work schedule off to later hours in the day will
pay dividends. All employees, in any organization,
prefer to work for superiors who show an interest in
their efforts and follow through by recognizing them
accordingly.

     When visiting public school classrooms in this
country, one soon discovers that teaching practices
have changed over the years. Gone are the days of
rapped knuckles, dunce caps, and, in most schools, the
bolted down desks. But the children are still entering
the classrooms each fall ready to be motivated to

"We consider effective
teaching a vital link
in the reform process.
The reason is clear:
Without good teaching,
other reform efforts--
school redesign,
curriculum reform--
are largely irrelevant."
--Charles DeRiemer,
Executive Director
Southwestern Bell
Foundation

learn. Students desire and expect discipline. A
teacher who tries to "become one of them" is usually
asking for trouble. Ask students and the majority will
tell you so. They can pick up a weak teacher the first
day of school. That is why that first day is so
important for a beginning or experienced teacher. When
a beginning teacher walks into the classroom for the
first time to face twenty-five ninth grade students and
begins by writing his name on the chalkboard and breaks
the chalk doing so, he had better have a good comeback.
Students will say to themselves, "He has gone through
four years of college and doesn't even know how to use
the chalk!" Believe it or not, the first ten to
fifteen minutes in the classroom for a beginning
teacher are the most critical. The teacher who
survives the initial introductory stage is on the way
to completing the first successful day in a teaching
career with only 179 more to go in the first year.

The way a teacher walks, speaks (voice pitch,
etc.), dresses, and uses non-verbal communications, eye
contact and posture are vital in the beginning life of
a new teacher, especially at the junior and senior high
levels. Students have their radar antennas out as soon
as Miss Jones enters the classroom. The stage is set
for acceptance or rejection. One mistake and students
will let you know immediately. I have seen beginning
teachers in tears at the end of the first day. They
usually say, "No one told me it was going to be like
this." Absolutely no one told them (not even their
college professors). Consequently, many are not prepared for the real world of teaching. Very few understand there are twenty-five or more individual behavior
patterns sitting in those seats. No two students are
alike. They all bring their emotional baggage from
home to the school. I don't care how they are grouped
or what criteria is used, each student is unique.

If the behavior of a student clashes with value
systems of a teacher, trouble begins to brew. Teachers
can't call for the x-ray machine, take a picture, diagnose, and then operate. Teaching involves changing
human behavior in classrooms. Attempts to diagnose a
student's learning problem by observation and pencil-
paper tests can be subjective. Special education is a
good example. Not so many years ago, children diagnosed

as learning disabled were soon forgotten. Severely mentally retarded children were treated as castaways. It was sad.

Fortunately with improved diagnosic methods, children with learning and physical disabilities are now being offered special treatment in our public and special schools. Outstanding work is being done for these students by dedicated special education teachers. I had the opportunity to visit the Great Falls (Montana) Public Schools special education complex and was amazed as I observed their diagnostic procedures for exceptional children. The director gave me a tour and showed a very comprehensive, professional team approach in diagnosis and instruction. One can only go so far in finding things out about the learning and mental disorders of a student. We have heard about the stigma of branding a student as L.D. (Learning Disabled) or B.D. (Behavioral Disorder), when in truth they never were a L.D. or B.D. student.

Too often when a student misbehaves or becomes disruptive in a classroom, the teacher immediately writes up a "referral" to have the child tested, claiming he is not normal and should be placed in a special learning environment. Translated, this implies that the student is a threat, and the teacher wants him out of the classroom.

Current research into right and left brain hemisphere functions is a step forward in attempting to objectively diagnose a student's overall potential to function in his environment. However, there is still much in the way of practical application that needs to be done while research continues.

Mr. Stuart Shoger, a veteran board of education member for the Aurora East School District, was among the pioneers in Innate Aptitude Testing. He was dedicated to studying measurement and findings of inborn traits. His interest in the topic centered around diagnosing an individual's innate abilities so that they could be properly counseled into various vocational areas. He was concerned that people go through life without finding out what their innate abilities are and, consequently, fumble through job after job

never really being successful. Shoger pointed out the
importance of innate testing at the junior high level.
He felt it was important for students, early in their
education, to be informed of their potential innate
abilities. He was concerned that students were not
being counseled properly and, therefore, ended up
graduating from high school or even college not knowing
what they wanted to do because they were not made aware
of their innate talents. The choice to pursue research
that is directed towards brain hemisphere research and
indigenous trait testing is vital. It will cost money
for trained professionals to conduct such testing
practices, but the funds will be money well spent and
certainly will serve to help teachers and assist students in their career decisions later on.

To take the innate trait testing idea one step
further, Margaret E. Brodley in her book, <u>Your Natural
Gifts</u>, talked about the innate aptitude that makes for
a good teacher.

> The top trait of a good teacher is
> ideaphoria...A teacher needs an abundant
> flow of ideas to formulate new projects,
> and stimulating assignments to keep the
> students interested. The teacher who
> lacks the trait usually fails at
> teaching; too often he leads a dull and
> bored class. And unless he has the
> aptitude, he too can fall into a rut
> teaching the same thing over and over in
> the same way. The satirist Juvenal put
> it this way: "It is repetition, like
> cabbage served at every meal, that wears
> out the schoolmaster's life."

In his study entitled <u>How to Get an 'A': Be Neat,
Be First, Change Your Name,</u> Clinton Chase, an education
professor at Indiana University, found evidence that
scores on essay tests are affected by a whole flock of
variables that are not related to the content of the
answers. Chase pointed out that names make a difference. Kim and Julie are more likely to receive higher
marks than Ethel or Maude. Neatness does count, and
the quality of handwriting and grammar affect the test
scores regardless of the content of the answers. More

interesting, I believe, is what Chase had to report about the position of a student's test in the pile. Those on the bottom of the pile are more likely to end up at the top of the bell curve. This means, according to Chase, as teachers work their way through the pile, they tend to grade higher. (Students should place their papers on the bottom and hope the teacher doesn't reverse the pile!)

Although teachers spend hours grading papers and recording grades, there is no question but that test construction and evaluating techniques need improvement all the way from kindergarten through graduate school. Here are a few cases taken from the files I kept on teachers and college professors and their grading practices.

Grade	Result/Comments
Fifth Grade Math	Twenty-five problems (fractions); student missed two, Grade C. (no comments)
Eleventh Grade American Literature	Neatly written, answered question, five page essay report, Grade C. (no comments)
Graduate School History and Foundations of Education	"You answered the questions but not the way I wanted you to." Grade C-.
Ninth Grade Science	Thirty-five fill in the blanks, missed 15, Grade B+. (no comments)

These and other examples show there is little, if any, consistency in grading practices throughout our schools and colleges. Every teacher and professor does his own thing. Although I don't believe that grading practices should be uniform, I do believe that every teacher and professor should be required to take a course in educational statistics and measurement and that administrators and department chairpersons, as well as deans, supervise grading practices within their respective departments and buildings. I have had teachers admit to me, after confronting them with poor grading practices stemming from complaints brought on by students and parents, that the reason was "they didn't feel good that day" or "they wanted to get even with the class." There is no excuse for such action or defense. Consequently, students become discouraged and more than one will say, "What is the use of trying. The highest grade I can get in the class is a 'C.' Mr./Mrs./Dr. 'so and so' doesn't believe in giving above a 'C' on a test." Teachers should not see how difficult they can make their class for students, but how they can motivate and challenge students to achieve. Any worthwhile dropout study should begin by studying the grading practices of teachers. Good teachers motivate their students through positive grading practices.

Albert Shanker, President of the 600,000 member American Association of Teachers, speaking before a union convention in Washington several years ago, asked teachers to take their place next to doctors and lawyers with self-governance and peer review. Shanker was asking teachers to become more professional. He cited the Rand Corporation study showing that the most able teachers leave the profession soonest and that the worst teachers stay the longest. Shanker admitted there are incompetent teachers as well as competent teachers with everything between these two extremes. He insists that teachers must begin policing their own ranks.

At the University of Chicago Graduate School of Education, extensive studies have been done on teacher expectations and student achievement. One study involved citing names of students to help probe hidden attitudes of the teacher. At the end of a school day, the researchers took the teachers out of their classrooms one by one and said, "Name all the boys in your classroom in any order you want." Then they asked the teachers to name all the girls in the classroom. The intent was to focus in on the children named first by the teachers and those named last and then go into the classroom and observe the teacher interacting with

"The purpose of
evaluation is to
increase performance,
increase professional
growth, and
remove deadwood."

those children. They discovered that often the teachers, after having taught the class for eight months, couldn't name all of the students twenty minutes after they left the classroom for the day. The researchers then took the children named first and the children named last one by one. If Billy Scott were named first, they said, "Now let's pretend that I am another teacher and Billy is going to be transferred to my room; tell me about Billy." They did the same thing for the boy named last, the girl named first, and the girl named last. The difference was striking. Much more was said about the first-named child than about the last-named child. Secondly, there was much more emotional involvement with the first-named child. They found comments such as "Oh, I really like Hilda," or "Billy's such a pain in the neck." Descriptions of the last-named child were much briefer, more passive, more uninvolved. The boys named first tended to be problems and the girls named first tended to be favorites. When the teachers were shown the results of the inquiry, they said the information was helpful. It not only pointed out children who were on the periphery of their teaching consciousness, it also forced them to examine why (Jackson, p. 46).

George Klemp, a psychologist with McBer and Co., Boston, said his company studied the traits of good and poor teachers, as measured by the achievement of students. "The most marked difference between good and bad teachers is in the trait of positive expectations," he said. "The good teachers believe their students will succeed...and the others have a low opinion of them." The other key trait separating the two is "group management skills - the ability to know where the students are and to be sensitive to their feelings." A certain level of knowledge is needed, he said, but "higher levels of knowledge do not predict superior performance" (Education U.S.A., p. 241).

Good teaching demands time, energy and patience. Careful planning must go into each day. In my teaching, I routinely ask myself what can I do tomorrow that I haven't done before? What things can I do that will turn my students on to learning regardless of race, color, sex and mental ability?

Good teachers can teach and teach well. In talking with parents on occasions, the topic of their favorite teacher would come up. "I remember Mrs. Gibbs. She was a no-nonsense teacher and we learned," one would say. "They don't have teachers like they used to," another voice would say. Well, I am sure that Mrs. Gibbs and others were good teachers in their day. The question is how would Mrs. Gibbs and others do in today's world of public education? Times have changed and education is a reflection of happenings and trends in society.

The trouble with today's world of public school teaching is that societal demands and changes have taken their toll on classroom teachers.

The word dedication will raise some teachers' eyebrows for they will tell you the main test is survival, especially in some of our inner city schools. Teachers who follow survival practices are only concerned where the train is taking them today, not where their students will be traveling in the future. The neat green plants on windows in teachers' class-rooms of yesterday have all but disappeared. Now they are replaced with enclosed brick and mortar to reduce energy costs. Gone are the days of the "Pledge Allegiance to the Flag" in many of our schools. Individual student aggressiveness and student group protests have surfaced during the last twenty years. Teacher strikes have replaced the once peaceful environment of the opening day of school. Teacher absenteeism has become an increasing problem. Teacher evaluation systems continue to be primarily checklists - a checklist that principals can easily fill out and do little to enhance professional growth and the improvement of instruction. In the Rand Corporation's Rand Checklist in a report titled "Teacher Evaluation: A Study of Effective Practices," that was conducted in 1988, concluded that four districts - Salt Lake City, Utah; Lake Washington, Washington; Toledo, Ohio; and Greenwich, Connecticut - "were best able to identify incompetent teachers and subsequently improve teacher performance." These four school systems were judged "exemplary" because (1) the school districts provided the resources to carry out the process, (2) evaluations were competent, (3) administrators and teachers worked

side by side in the development of the programs, and
(4) the system related to local, district and community
educational characteristics. School districts across
the country are deeply concerned about being forced to
hire "the least academically qualified" personnel.
Better salaries elsewhere, low pay, lack of administrative support, bureaucracy, and changing student
behavior are among the main causes for a dwindling
teacher corps in our public schools today.

Federal and state mandates and intervention in
what is to be taught and for how long have replaced the
once cherished possession of local control and decision
making. All in all, public education has changed and
so has the teaching profession. We can talk reform
about public education until we're blue in the face,
but nothing is going to happen unless there is a choice
made toward improving the teaching environment for the
teachers.

Capable, consistent supervision of the teaching
staff is needed. Teacher unions and school officials
must recognize this and be willing to sit down side by
side, utilizing their combined talents to update evaluation procedures so that the outcomes reward the good
performance and remove the "deadwood." Objective, individual, goal-oriented evaluation procedures focusing
on specific measurable outcomes can do this. Making
the choice to evaluate personnel this way is, by far,
the most accountable approach when it comes to upgrading the profession and raising educational standards.
There is no question that good teachers deserve better
salaries. The question is, how do you go about con-
vincing school boards and the local taxpayers that
increased salaries will result in better teaching?
Answer: Through a well-designed evaluation program
that objectively reveals who can teach and who cannot
teach.

Paralleling the need for effective evaluation of
personnel is the topic of teacher tenure. The "pros
and cons" of tenure must be dealt with by all
educational parties and lawmakers. Questions need to
be brought out and answered, including what is the
purpose of tenure? Does having it improve teaching?
Who benefits from it? Does tenure protect the weak

teachers? The choice to remove tenure and substitute much higher salaries as a trade-off must become a point of discussion between teachers and school boards. If tenure serves to improve instruction and help students learn better, then we ought to keep the process; however, needing tenure to protect a teacher against the evil practices of administrators is a tune that has been over-played.

The choice must be made to protect good teaching in our public schools and nourish it if future generations are going to move our country forward. It is impossible to expect teachers to pick the future Einsteins of tomorrow, but we can and should expect a classroom environment that encourages and motivates the majority of students to learn. In other words, we want as much cream as possible to rise to the top in our classrooms. Maintaining and protecting weak links in any profession will certainly weaken the bond of professionalism and eventually cause the profession to crumble. This must not happen to our public schools. The cure is to make the choice to train, maintain, encourage, and expand the corps of teachers in our public schools who can teach and teach effectively. The future of our country rests in the classroom under their guidance. Without teachers, we have no other professions.

Chapter 4

What About School Boards?

"Now, perhaps as no other time in recent history, school boards, superintendents, and everyone associated with public education need to close ranks and direct efforts toward the goal of preserving the right of every student to a free public education. ...
Tension is inevitable because of the differences in our functions within the school system. After nearly 25 years as a school board member, I finally believe in one simple rule: a school board should ensure that the superintendent has enough authority to carry out his or her designated responsibilities, and the superintendent should assure the board that the responsibilities designated are, in fact, being met. ...
Board members and superintendents, as members of the same management team, sometimes have individual differences that pale in comparison with the many things on which they agree, share, and have in common. Remember that small annoyances tend to divide people. Major crises often draw them together.
The years ahead will require the best that is in us. Our example will set the pace and patterns for all within and outside the schools who look to us for leadership.
We must rise to the challenge that is our tradition, our common desire, and our commitment."

--Robert Haderlein
The American School
Board Journal

Robert Haderlein, Past President of the National School Boards Association, effectively states the case for choosing positive, vision-oriented leaders at top-level management positions in our public school districts and for electing supportive, dedicated persons to support decisions.

My first working experience with a school board came in 1971 when I was appointed Director of Curriculum in a rural school district in Ohio. The first thing I noticed among the five-member board was that they all were interested in quality education. However, each had a different philosophy on how that goal should be reached. It took a great deal of "show and tell" presentations to convince them that we educators knew something about how to run a school district, especially in the area of instruction.

My next experience with school boards came in 1973 when a national search was conducted by the Upper Darby School District, a suburban school system near Philadelphia, seeking an assistant superintendent of schools. I was selected for the position. During my second month on the job, the Board of Education asked me to chair a special committee consisting of professional staff, lay citizens, and a school board member. Our committee was to determine if there was a need to build a third junior high school near the site of the present (older) structure. After much study and investigation, the committee decided unanimously that it would be in the best interest of the students and the future of the school district to build a new junior high school. The school was to contain innovative individualized teaching programs (7-9) and be open to the public for expanded adult educational programs during the day as well as in the evening. The recommendation was brought before the board of education and a vote was taken approving the committee's recommendation to build the school. We then proceeded to move toward the goal. However, several months later, a financial crisis hit the school district. Not only was funding reduced, local income fell behind predictions, and a decline in student enrollment was forecast for the future. Faced with this dilemma, the school board convened and voted by a 5-3 margin to reverse its earlier decision. It was decided not to build the new school but instead, to close the existing building and bus all students to the two remaining junior high schools. Such action caused furor between parents of the community and the board of education. Demonstrations occurred all over the school district, and board of education meetings had standing room only. Residents of the affected school took legal action against the board of education to prevent the closing of "their" junior high school. The case ended up going to court, and the judge enjoined the school district from closing the school pending a hearing. The subsequent events became even more interesting.

As chairperson of the committee that recommended the building of a new school, I was served a subpoena on behalf of the plaintiffs. The nine-member school board and the superintendent were named as defendents in the case. I was caught in the crossfire! After one year in a new position, I was about to testify, under oath, on behalf of a group of concerned citizens against the board of education which hired me and the superintendent of schools to whom I directly reported! The case was heard in the Common Pleas Court. I can remember both attorneys advising me of the manner they preferred in responding to their questions. The school board's attorney suggested I keep my comments at a low key, while the citizens' attorney wanted me to exert real gusto when my remarks addressed the issue of why the committee recommended the building of a new school. In addition to my testimony supporting the building of the new school, three junior high school principals also testified in favor of the new construction. Finally after a week of testimony and listening to a variety of witnesses (including the superintendent, school board members, teachers, parents, citizens, and the mayor of the village), the judge ruled in favor of the citizens prohibiting the board of education from closing the school and permitted the building of the new school. In his decision the judge stated that his opinion was primarily based upon "the testimony of Dr. Fuhr and the report of the committee which recommended new site construction to insure better education for the students." Later, the board of education appealed the case to the Appellate Court of Pennsylvania which reversed the decision of the Common Pleas Court and ruled in favor of the school district giving permission to close the junior high school. This is just one story of many which illustrates the constant turmoil and frustration that confronts school boards in this country, even when their intentions and purposes are honorable.

A brief look at the history of school administration reveals school boards have not been immune to controversy in the past. The late 1800's and early 1900's found school boards and superintendents at odds with local citizenry in this country, but the issues and conflicts did not carry the intensity that occurs in present times.

The main difference, as I see it, between the past and present, is that today's brand of controversy affects a larger segment of the school community. Everyone gets into the act (for example, when there is discussion of salary for personnel, especially the superintendent's salary). Superintendents are demanding higher salaries and benefits because they want job security. One school district I know of has gone through six superintendents in the last eleven years. Even though the salary is competitive, good, potential candidates are scared off from applying because of the job history of their predecessors.

Once while having a small repair done on my fishing boat, I noticed a large semi-trailer truck full of outboard motors being unloaded. I decided to give the dealer a hand and, in the process, struck up a conversation with the truck driver who was from Wisconsin. He asked me what I did, and I told him I was a school superintendent. He laughed and said, "I wouldn't have your job no matter what they paid me. All the 'crap' you guys have to take from this group and that group isn't worth all the money they would pay me." I cheerfully told him that was what made the job interesting. Then the fellow said, "I have a brother who is on the school board at a rural community in northern Wisconsin. They have one meeting a month, which usually lasts about an hour or two at the most." He went on to state that the board members supported the superintendent and things went rather smoothly. I was informed that the present superintendent had been there for a number of years but would be retiring next

"School boards
need members
to be leaders,
not insurgents."

year. "What is your name again?" I told him, and he
said, "Good fishing lakes up there and I will mention
to my brother that I met you and if you're interested,
here is his name." He wrote down his brother's name
and I thanked him for the information. Although I am
always tempted to go where there is good fishing, I was
satisfied in my position at the time and was not that
anxious to consider a change. But I've often thought
about that school board and others that meet once a
month for one or two hours. School administrators,
especially superintendents, cherish the thought of such
an operation, knowing, however, that the "grass is not
always greener on the other side," regardless of the
size of the school system.

My experiences in public education include some
sixty cases of litigation over a span of eighteen
years. I was either a plaintiff or defendant in cases
concerned with desegregation and busing, teacher/prin-
cipal dismissal suits, teacher strikes, and personnel
matters dealing with the violation of an employee's
rights. In addition, there have been parent/student
suits of various nature. These experiences and those
of my colleagues have made me even more convinced that
superintendents and school boards must choose to work
together as a team. The distractions encountered by
our school leaders in today's world of public school
administration are numerous. Having to cope with the
added burden of board and administrator divisiveness
weakens one's ability to effectively deal with the
distractions.

In the March 1982 issue of the American School
Board Journal, Gordon Cawelte, who served as Executive
Director of the Association for Supervision and
Curriculum Development in Washington, D.C., provided
the results of a survey he conducted on how big city
superintendents perceive their school boards. Cawelte
stated:

> "Whether they rated their boards
> high or low, superintendents volunteered
> some wide-ranging criticism about their
> board's conduct. Typical of their major
> concerns were comments such as these:
> - "This board is overly responsive to
>   criticism on specific problems or to

> pressure groups."
> - "Most of them have managed nothing
> more than a checkbook; our budget is
> beyond their grasp."
> - "They are not well informed enough
> to deal with complex issues."
>
> "Several superintendents reported
> the well-known split-vote phenomenon is a
> regular pattern that encouraged citizens
> to go to individual board members who
> supported the citizens specific point of
> view."

Cawelte's study then asked superintendents to identify board member types who would hinder the ability to reach consensus on various issues.

> "The types most frequently identified
> by superintendents: single issue board
> members (46% of superintendents responded
> that such board members make formulating
> decisions difficult); politically
> ambitious board members (46%); board
> members who are openly responsive to the
> needs of their own geographic area of the
> school district (44%); and board members
> who are overly responsive to teacher
> viewpoints (42%)."

Certainly, one must look at the other side of the coin as well. In managing school districts, superintendents and other top-level school administrators can create their own problems. There are times when blame directed towards central office administrators regarding (1) poor communications, (2) bypassing the board on major issues, and (3) failing to make decisions is justified. Good strong decisive leadership will serve to reduce tension between the board of education and the administration.

School districts say they need strong leadership at the board of education level, but indecisive leaders are still being appointed or voted in. The need to choose competent board of education personnel in our public school systems is paramount. There are more than 15,000 local school boards in this country with over 95,000 members with 90% being elected by the vote of local communities. Because of the tremendous turn-over year after year, there are always new personalities with whom superintendents must deal.

Professor Robert E. Wilson of Kent State University, in a 1980 study, did some investigating between superintendents who are successful and those that come, as Wilson labeled them, "untracked."

Wilson studied sixteen district superintendents who were identified as being successful. Then he studied nineteen other superintendents that had experienced either non-renewal of contract, retired under pressure, took a job elsewhere, or left the superintendency altogether. Wilson discovered that:

- Untracked superintendents experienced more and longer board meetings;
- In eight of the districts, one or more members of the board had run "to get the superintendent";
- In two districts candidates sought revenge against the superintendent for failing to employ certain persons as teachers;
- More than two-thirds of the board members favoring nonrenewal of the superin-tendent's contract were serving a first term on the board. (Wilson concluded the findings support the belief that approx-imately half of the board members in the study ran for their job in order "to get the superintendent");
- Six of the untracked superintendents never were given a reason for nonrenewal;
- Board conditions that created superinten-dent problems included a divided board and collusion of one or more members with union leaders or board treasurer (from Robert Olds, Illinois School Board Journal).

Wilson stated that in eleven of the nineteen districts, one member was identified as strong enough

to influence a majority of membership to his way of
thinking on nearly all important issues. Drawing
conclusions from his study, Wilson said, "from my
familiarity with hundreds of school superintendents
over the years, I was convinced that those sixteen most
successful superintendents, superb as they are, were
not that much different in personal characteristics or
methods of operation from many others who were not
ranked so highly. They simply had a board that
understood their role, teamwork, and the role of the
superintendent" (Olds, pp. 20-21).

The question over whether school board members
should be elected or appointed is not, in my opinion,
the issue. The issue is whether or not board members
are qualified? Do they bring to the position management expertise as well as first-hand knowledge and
experience of public education? I would suggest all
candidates seeking a seat on the board of education be
required to meet the following requirements:

1. Each must have substitute taught one
   day at an elementary and secondary
   school in their school district
   within one year prior to announcing
   candidacy. All members must continue to do this annually as long
   as they serve on the board of
   education.

2. Each must provide evidence of
   understanding and knowledge on
   techniques of effective management,
   and attend at least one conference
   or workshop a year to stay abreast
   of current management trends and
   issues.

3. Each should also visit schools and
   talk with teachers and administrators to demonstrate a commitment
   to education.

4. Each must present an acceptable
   score on statewide "local school
   district operations test," developed
   and administered by the state board
   of education.

We know that in the business world a company must have teamwork at the top and top-caliber management personnel, if the business is to succeed and make a profit. The board of directors of any successful corporation must clearly understand the role of management as distinguished from their own duties and responsibilities.

The same is true in the operation of a school district. Boards of education must assume the major responsibility for policy making but give the support and authority to the superintendent and staff to run the school district. Too many battles are fought over insignificant matters that should have been settled before they mushroomed out of proportion. As the Wilson study indicated, crusades are waged between individual board of education members and the superintendent. There have been too many excellent superintendents' reputations ruined over charges that were later proven false. Once a case "hits the press," it is difficult for a superintendent to regain his credibility and some will be subject to dismissal or resignation. Back in 1976, Dr. Paul Briggs, among the longest-termed big-city superintendents in the nation at the time, told a group of Ohio administrators, "school managers have many resemblances to endangered wildlife in that their breeding grounds have been fouled up, those selected for survival are the least likely to survive, and it is open season all year around." The Cleveland superintendent added, "When he is bagged, the superintendent isn't even considered a prize" (Information Legislative Service, p. 3).

Teachers closely watch the happenings between the school boards and top-level school administrators. When there is bickering and "sneak attacks" going on, the troops become restless. They develop a feeling of insecurity and frustration causing teacher unions to become stronger within the affected school system. Eventually, each distinct personnel group in the school district begins to form separate entities; the teachers have their group; the custodians, theirs; secretaries form their group. Consequently, all these groups spend time trying to find out what is going on and protecting their own turf from mismanagement practices. The outcome is a divided district infused with low morale, increased student discipline problems, and declining performance.

The 20th Annual Gallop Poll conducted in 1988 surveyed communities and their attitudes toward public education. People in the sample were asked to grade public schools in the nation as a whole:

	National Totals %	No.C'dren in School %	Pub.Sch. Parents %	Nonpublic Sch.Parents %
A-rating	3	2	3	2
B-rating	20	19	22	16
C-rating	48	46	52	57
D-rating	13	13	12	16
Fail	3	4	2	2
Don't Know	13	16	9	7

Although it was pointed out in the survey that the more familiar the "grader" was with his local schools, the higher the ratings. Nevertheless, the grades were not impressive.

It is my belief that part of the problem regarding how parents view schools throughout this country has much to do with media reporting of the "goings on" between school boards and superintendents, between school boards and teachers, and between school board members themselves. Positive stories do not sell newspapers. Teacher assault cases, teachers/administrators being shot, vandalism, gang warfare, teacher strikes, closing of a school, spectators and coaches being fired upon at our football games, students killed by a parent, drug overdose, financial cutbacks, and other sensational headlines take precedent over the 95% of the positive things that occur in our modern-day public schools. When it comes to public education, media reporting plays a major role in shaping the beliefs of the public. Subsequently, negative media coverage leads to negative beliefs by the reader resulting in negative attitudes toward our public educational system. We are a society curious about sensational happenings. The majority of our public schools in this country are doing a fine job of providing an account-

"School board members always need to ask themselves: Are we sticking to policy making or are we crossing over into administration?"

able educational package to their students; unfortunately, the positive happenings frequently get edited out of local, state, and national media coverage.

It is the responsibility of the school board to publicize and publicly support its schools and to convey to the general public that the goal of the board and the total school system is teamwork.

In 1976 a ten-year study on why superintendents get fired appeared in the June issue of The Michigan School Board Journal. The following findings pertain only to what a superintendent may do to encourage dismissal from the position.

    (1) Develop a poor relationship with the board of education by
       (a) refusal to seek and accept criticism,
       (b) the lack of a harmonious working relationship with the board,
       (c) failure to support board policy and follow instructions.
    (2) Refuse to permit the board of education to evaluate the superintendent annually in a formal written manner. Only eight (13 percent) of the 60 superintendents included in the data analysis were evaluated by the board of education in a formal written manner at least annually. All others were evaluated in one of three ways: a written manner less often than annually, a verbal manner, or not evaluated at all.
    (3) Fail to cultivate the respect of his personnel. Twenty-six (43 percent) of the 60 superintendents were appraised by board members as not having the respect of school personnel and this, therefore, was a "partial reason for release." School personnel are members of the community and eventually they will influence members of the board of education.

(4) Fail to provide adequate communications. The failure to communicate
properly with school personnel,
board of education members, and the
community was listed as a "partial
reason for release" for 27 (45
percent) of the 60 superintendents.

(5) Accept a position where the local
board of education screens the
applicants and selects the candidate
without assistance from consultants
out of the district. There was a
significant relationship between the
dismissal or encouragement of a
superintendent to leave and the
procedure utilized in the selection
process. Thirty-nine (65 percent)
of the 60 superintendents were
selected in a manner in which the
local board of education secured no
assistance in the selection process
from university placement officials
or outside consultants.

(6) Show a lack of concern about the
size of the student enrollment of
the school district. The data
indicated that the size of the
school district was a significant
factor in release of Michigan school
superintendents. The conclusions
drawn from the study indicated that
superintendents of school districts
with student enrollments of 2,501 to
5,000 and of those with over 10,000
students were most susceptible to
release. Those superintendents of
school districts with student
enrollments of 1,000 or less and of
those districts with from 5,000 to
10,000 students were least susceptible to release.

(7) Fail to strive to become more
proficient in the areas of interpersonal relationships. Few
Michigan school superintendents were
released for performing poorly in

the area of business and finance or
in the area of educational leadership. It was in the area of interpersonal relationships that the
underlying reason for release
exists.

Other significant facts brought out by the ten-
year Michigan study indicated conflict between superintendents and boards of education. Some of these facts
were that

- The release of Michigan school
  superintendents had increased
  significantly. Seventy percent of
  the cases included in the study
  occurred during a five-year period
  (1971-76).
- Most of these Michigan school
  superintendents were released with
  short advance notice. Fifty-four
  (90 percent) of the 60 superintendents were given six months or
  less advance notice, with nine (15
  percent) given no advance notice at
  all.
- The superintendent's role as a chief
  negotiator for management was not a
  significant factor in the release of
  Michigan superintendents.
- Performance in the areas of business
  and finance was not a significant
  factor in the release.
- The percentage of minority students
  enrolled in the school district was
  not a significant factor in the
  release of Michigan school
  superintendents.
- Geographic location of a school
  district in Michigan was not a
  significant factor in the release of
  the superintendents.

The Michigan study illustrated what continues
today between superintendents and boards of education.
As was pointed out in the study, there was incon-
sistency in the evaluation of superintendents by boards

"Long-range
planning is the
link to effective
decision making."

of education throughout the state. Evaluation of personnel should always be a consistent and objective process with the understanding that the end result should be increased professional growth and performance.

The National School Boards Association, in partnership with member state school boards associations, published an article in 1982 entitled "Becoming a Better Board Member." The report highlighted the following points in the evaluation process between boards of education and superintendents:

- Good practice starts at the top. It begins with the board and the board starts with self-evaluation.
- Combine the evaluation of the superintendent with that of the board and its policies.
- The board evaluation should be constructive. It should be a tool that is both positive and helpful, assessing both the strengths and weaknesses of a board. It should also provide a systematic process by which the members of a board can improve their performance.
- Board members should develop the standards that measure their relationship with the superintendent. These standards should include how the board effectively plans, makes decisions, and sets policy. Evaluation at the end of the year should be based on what the board planned to do at the beginning of the year.
- In most communities, the public is of little help in evaluating the board of education because the public doesn't know what the board does.
- A composite picture of the board's strengths and weaknesses is best. Each board member should complete an evaluation form independently. Then

the board as a whole should meet to
compare and discuss results.

A study conducted by the Institute for Educational
Leadership in Washington, D.C., reported in the Phi
Delta Kappan (September 1987) that the majority of
school boards do not assess their performance. Unfortunately, self-evaluation is the exception rather
than the rule.

If the board of education expects the superintendent to be an effective administrator, then the board
must set the example by first being accountable themselves. Not only must an annual self-assessment be
done, but boards of education must do what successful
corporate trustees do:

- Set goals
- Grow professionally
- Communicate effectively
- Delegate wisely
- Motivate personnel to achieve.

The old saying "What is good for the goose is also
good for the gander" applies. Teamwork and understanding must exist at the top if there is to be a
successful marriage between boards of education and
their chief executive officer. Too many superintendents fail to work with their respective boards of
education in establishing annual priorities. The outcome is that superintendents deal in what motivational
expert Zig Zigler in See You At The Top refers to as
"wandering generalities" rather than in "meaningful
specifics."

Many school boards in this country fail to
establish a game plan with goals and guidelines for the
school district to follow. Instead of running full
speed ahead, many school systems make the choice to
operate in neutral gear or, in some cases, in reverse.
No one is taking charge. Leadership is lacking or
being destroyed by those who are supposed to be
providing it in the school systems. The following
exerpt is from the September 1988 issue of The School
Administrator, in which I wrote an article entitled
"Ten Best Ways to Kill Leadership." Based on

observations of present school district management problems, I thought it was time someone addressed how leadership is being destroyed.

1. <u>Conduct annual evaluations based on generalities rather than meaningful specifics.</u> Remember that an evaluator must not give in to those experts who advocate individualized plans of evaluation which lend themselves to specific goal-setting formats. The key is to not let the evaluatee know what is expected of him. Then, when the evaluatee wanders around the school district in a daze not knowing where he stands, the evaluator can deliver a warning notice that performance is not up to par. This, of course, can open the door leading to dismissal. By keeping personnel in the dark, there is a good chance that leadership on the part of the management team will never surface. Remember, the goal is to keep them guessing!

2. <u>Keep praise at a low level</u>. The key here is watching what is said when the evaluatee performs at a high level of competency. Don't let employees know that the job was well done; they may become motivated. Electing not to respond to those employees who exert top performance can eventually cause a decay in their self-esteem which can lead to resignation or pursuit of employment in a school district where praise is aligned with top performance.

3. <u>Keep asking for detailed reports.</u> Demand constant feedback by requiring lengthy reports on issues that could otherwise be handled effectively with a "yes" or "no" answer. With all the present demands and challenges facing school officials, requiring detailed paperwork to accompany every decision and recommendation will prevent them from addressing the demands of their particular positions and will offer little time for them to lead a school effectively.

4. <u>Make sure meetings last a long time.</u> Drag out meetings with irrelevant questions and ask for more discussion before making decisions. Don't follow the agenda, and let anyone speak for as long as they like. Streamlined, well-organized meetings tend to foster incentive to do more than what is expected. The key is to keep having irrelevant meetings. This is an

excellent way to wipe out professional growth and will serve to speed up the burnout process.

5. Criticize performance in public. Knock out leadership in a person by embarrassing him in public. Put an employee on the defensive or engage him in a shouting match. A good time to do this is at a well-attended school board meeting. Many experts of management study call this "hitting below the belt," but to those devastators of leadership, it is known as "getting even."

6. Use the words, "I have been told by some that such and such happened." The key to this tactic is the word "some." The implication is the evaluator is dissatisfied with the evaluatee's performance, and "others" have voiced the same feelings. This is one of the best ways to undermine a person's self-esteem and help create distrust within the "team." Be prepared to answer the question, "Name the some." If this occurs, don't say who the "some" are. Instead, say that it is important to maintain confidentiality.

7. Play sneak attack. Lay traps and use camouflage which can't be easily seen or discovered by the employee. For example, leak information to "out-siders" relating to the results of a certain employee's evaluation or suggest twelve months ahead of time that someone's contract will not be renewed. Going behind the backs of employees in an attempt to discredit them will keep many good rising stars in school administration off the highway of success.

8. Expect perfection. Don't accept the notion that failure can lead to success. If that happens, people will begin succeeding from their failures through words of encouragement. Expecting perfection will put overloaded burdens on targeted employees who will eventually blow a fuse, resulting in a shut down of their performance. To realize success in this technique, have someone try to light a spark under them and their response is "What's the use?"

9. Turn down requests for professional growth and development. Inform the employee that the "fires" at home need to be tended and that wandering

off to some professional convention will look bad in the eyes of the public. Using taxpayers money to attend out-of-town conventions should be discouraged since there could be a chance that something might be gained; for example, leadership techniques could be brought back to your school district, implemented, and found to work.

          10. <u>Attempt to please everyone.</u> Going around trying to please everyone is known as "popularity management." Popularity management contaminates the roots of leadership in any organization. When a school administrator goes around praising everyone, including those who don't deserve it, those who are deserving become discouraged. Hard work, dedication, and determination--cornerstones of individual leadership--are put on equal footing with laziness, complaining, and poor performance. Praising those whose work is below par rates high on the list of excellent methods of destroying leadership.

       These ten ways to kill leadership and initiative can almost be guaranteed to work. Of course, reversing these methods will almost certainly bring out the best in school management personnel. The choice is one of deciding to promote leadership or destroy it!

       The need to set goals annually is a crucial requirement for boards of education. Transferring the goals into an action plan in order to judge performance of personnel is equally important. In addition, job descriptions for management personnel, which in some school districts are outdated or simply don't exist, should also be considered as part of the evaluation process. Writing down plans for reaching goals in specific terms, MBO (Management By Objectives) with timetables for completion, and being held accountable for the accomplishment of the plans is one of the best and fairest methods of evaluation, especially when those being evaluated have input into their design. All school boards in this country should choose to make their number one priority an annual assessment of their own effectiveness.

       The key in evaluating anyone's performance in management is to be specific. The more specific the format, the more chance of being objective. For example:

Goal:	Enhance Staff Morale
Objective:	Satisfactory performance will have been achieved by
(Wrong)	improving communications between teachers, principals, and the central office administrators.
Objective:	Satisfactory performance will have been achieved when a schedule is developed by
(Right)	October 1990 whereby central office administrators and school board members will visit two schools per month in order to improve communications between teachers, principals, and central office administrators.

Once the evaluation format is in place so that performance (be it of school board members or school administrators) can be judged effectively, the key question then becomes, "How do you get 'qualified' people to run for the school board?" Being what it is -- a thankless position with long hours, frustration and headaches -- what can be done to attract competent citizens to serve? Granted, there are the "do good-ers," the "crusaders," the "have all the answers" types who can't wait to assume a public office position such as serving on the school board. Often such people have gained popularity as spokespersons for an advocacy group. Unfortunately, many of these kind of individuals do run for election on school boards and are elected. It takes a dedicated individual to be an effective school board member--a person who is willing to make a commitment for team management and creative leadership and to sacrifice personal interests for the common interests. The following choices should be given consideration by any local community in order to attract competent people to be on its local school board:

- Choose individuals who are familiar
  with public education;
- Choose individuals who are versed in
  effective management practices;
- Choose individuals who are long on
  dedication;
- Choose individuals who possess the
  skills needed in carrying out
  effective human relation practices;
- Choose individuals who are decision
  makers.

Throughout the country there are good school boards exerting excellent leadership and management practices within their school systems. In such cases, a destination has been plotted with a vision toward the future. School board meetings run effectively are piloted by individuals who know how to run efficient meetings.

David Kipp, superintendent of schools in Colorado, wrote an article in the March 1982 issue of the <u>American School Board Journal</u> listing the following kinds of school board members that drive superintendents crazy:

- <u>The know-it-alls:</u> These are board
  members who think they know all
  there is to know about managing
  schools without the benefit of experience or professional advice.
  When they run for the board, their
  campaign slogan always is "Let's
  straighten out the schools."

- <u>The ax-grinders:</u> These board
  members get onto the school board
  with one purpose in mind: to
  promote their special interest, be
  it basketball, the basics, or
  busing.

- <u>The jellyfish:</u> Board members of
  this type have chocolate eclairs
  where backbones belong. As soon as
  one of them receives a complaint

"Employees in a school
district won't follow
their leaders unless
they know their
leaders care for them."

about the schools, he's on the
telephone to the superintendent
demanding "a full explanation."
They are squeamish about backing the
administration in disputes with
employees or students, and they are
the first to give in to pressure
from special-interest groups.

· The joiners: These board members
are adept at spotting education
trends and leading the parade right
onto the bandwagon. They have
extremely short memories when their
bright ideas begin to dim.

· The ward-heelers: These are board
members who want - demand - special
favors for their friends, children,
relatives, business colleagues.
Need a building contractor for a new
school? They know one. Have an
opening on the cheerleading squad?
Their daughters are ready and
leaping.

· The personnel directors: These
board members want to interview and
hire all teachers in the school
system...They love power over the
superintendent.

· The motor mouths: These are vocal
board members who volunteer to the
press or anyone else, explanations
for why the board acted as it did on
a matter.

Probably anyone who has served as, or is presently
serving as, a superintendent of schools can identify
various board members as fitting into one of Kipp's
classifications.

As I see it, board members, in turn, have their
classifications of superintendents:

• The over-the-hill person: These are superintendents that currently have one goal in mind and only one: Survive until retirement. Afraid to "rock the boat," these superintendents throw the major responsibility of decision making and policy enforcement to the board. They are very competent in handling travel arrangements for board members desiring to attend state and national conventions.

• The jock: These superintendents have come up through the ranks in a school district as teacher, guidance counselor, coach, principal, assistant superintendent, superintendent. Lacking understanding about instructional program development, their emphasis is on the "good old days." They impress others by attending athletic events and meeting former players. Every home game is like an alumni weekend where everyone shares stories with his former coach now turned superintendent.

• The paper producer: These types of superintendents drive board members up a wall with paper correspondence. Every form of activity occurring in the school district from sun up to sun down, seven days a week, fifty-two weeks a year is sent out in memo form. Board members feel obligated to read what they receive just in case it might be important. Such correspondence is carried out under the umbrella known as effective, ongoing communications. Superintendents who fall into this category have been known to make arrangements to have the press continue grinding out irrelevant articles while they are on vacation or on an extended leave of absence.

- <u>The silent one</u>: Superintendents in this category often confuse board members because they say little if anything at board meetings unless asked, and then their reply is vague. Board members at times question themselves whether their superintendent is "dead or alive." This type of superintendent rarely ventures beyond the office and decision making is mostly left to other members of the administrative staff.

- <u>The change agent</u>: These superintendents keep board members in a state of confusion and turmoil. They keep the district churning by continuously presenting for approval a bombardment of changes effecting all major operations of the school district. They offer a good example of the school district running full speed ahead but in neutral. Many of the changes recommended to the board and approved are never carried out.

- <u>The debonair executive</u>: These superintendents project the Madison Avenue image. Everyone takes notice at the board meetings since the latest fashion in men's/women's apparel will be on display. Superintendents in this category have their offices professionally decorated, drive a late model car, and spend more time with the "movers and pillars" of the community than with the persons to whom they are responsible.

There are as many different types of board members as superintendents, to be sure. Because of the many kinds of personalities that must be dealt with, there

will always be misunderstandings and disagreements.
Healthy confrontation is good and is sometimes the only
way to resolve conflict. The important thing that must
happen is that the school boards must choose to grant
superintendents authority and support to carry out the
policies and responsibilities of the school district.
The board sets the policies; the superintendent makes
certain those policies are carried out. The buck
passing stops at the superintendent's desk.

Carrying out the policy decisions made by the
school board takes positive leadership on the part of
the superintendent. Positive leaders address obsta-
cles, frustrations, and conflicts with a positive
attitude, seeing those situations as opportunities or
challenges rather than problems. Henry Ford once said,
"Getting together is the beginning. Working together
is progress. Staying together is success." Positive
leadership breeds the teamwork, cooperation, and
dedication to make things work. Teachers, support
staff, and the community will each do their part in
helping the goals and policies become a reality when
they observe positive, inspiring leadership at the top.
Evaluations of policies and of the staff must be done
with the motive being to improve professional growth.
Positive efforts on the part of the staff will be
rewarded by positive leaders. Pats on the back, thank-
you notes, and public affirmations must be earned and
passed on consistently. Positive competition among the
various school buildings to see who can address the
priorities during a given year with more success and
enthusiasm is healthy. Competition makes people want
to achieve as long as they first know what it is they
have to accomplish. With an atmosphere of trust and
respect between the board members and the superintendent, issues can be handled with the knowledge that
even in the midst of conflict the "team" will still be
intact when the issue is resolved. Positive handling
of issues will model the kind of teamwork that is
desired for the community and the teaching staff.
Having affirming, enthusiastic leadership at the top
will have a ripple effect throughout the school
district and the entire community.

The future of our public schools depends on making
the choice to have competent school administrators who

possess the skills of leadership and management. The best designed curriculum, instructional materials, and school buildings will not advance education in our public schools unless first there is healthy teamwork in place at the top levels of administration. According to management experts, one needs to incorporate 75% human relations and 25% job skills in top-level administrative positions if top performance is to be expected among the work force. Public affirmation of those who deserve it marks the good leader. What the public thinks of the schools is just as important as what the schools really are. An effective management team recognizes the importance of community support and also understands that such support can only come through a display of competent administration.

Although nothing has been mentioned about state boards of education, much of what has been said equally applies to state agencies. It is not my intent to minimize the importance of state boards of education. However, the choice must be made to have leadership that is aimed at promoting and providing quality education for our youth beginning at the local level. States that mandate programs and reforms from the top down deal a serious blow to creative leadership at the local level. It is true that too many local agencies have failed to exert decisive leadership in running their school districts. Therefore, state boards of education have had no choice but to step in and take charge when student achievement continually declines, teacher absenteeism increases, and there is a lack of supervision and accountability on the part of administrative personnel. Then legislators put the pressure on their respective state boards of education and departments of education to take over and mandate packages of educational reform. Local school districts then act as puppets with the strings controlled by state agencies. This practice is a mistake. Local school districts should be given local autonomy to achieve educational goals arrived at jointly with local and state officials within any given state. The guidelines for reform is then on the shoulders of local school boards and school administrators. They must assume responsibility for carrying out those guidelines.

Public education for the 21st century will improve
providing the choice is made by local boards of education to have competent school administrators serving at
the helm of the school district and by the public's
requiring that their school be populated with capable
people.   Such a choice will create school systems that
offer hope and encouragement for the future of all
students who daily enter our elementary and secondary
classrooms.

Chapter 5

Who's Teaching Our Teachers?

*"Faculties of education will not be able to
touch the lives of their students unless their
own lives have been touched - unless their
conception of education is reflected in the way
they teach as well as what they teach. ...*
*If schools of education are to turn out
men and women who not only know how to teach
but who are as well 'students of teaching,'
their program must have a far greater coherence
than most now have. ... To provide coherence in
this sense, the faculty must continuously ask
itself the question few faculties have asked:
What difference does it make that a teacher is
educated here, rather than somewhere else?*
*Faculties of education will have to do
more than that. The remaking of American
education requires, and will not be possible
without, a new kind of relationship between
colleges and universities on the one side,
and public schools on the other."*

--Charles Silberman
<u>Crisis in the Classroom</u>

The above view by Charles Silberman, taken from
<u>Crisis in the Classroom</u> (1970) regarding schools of
education, still holds true today. Take a look at the
following samples of vacancy notices taken from several
1984 issues of <u>The Chronicle of Higher Education</u> for

the position of Dean, Schools and Colleges of Education. Only the qualifications are listed and the name of the university or college has been omitted. I have arbitrarily assigned a rating 1 (low) to 5 (high) with relation to requiring "front line" experience as a public school administrator.

Administrative Positions
(Dean: School or College of Education)
Example 1.

Position: Dean, College of Education

Qualifications:
The Dean should have an earned doctorate and possess the qualifications necessary for rank of Professor. The Dean should be experienced in the development of resources necessary for the carrying out of the programs of the College. The Dean should demonstrate leadership, good communication skills, and have a broad view of education as a life long process.

Location: Southwestern United States
Type: University
Rating: 2+

Example 2.

Position: Dean, School of Education

Required Qualifications:
An earned doctorate in education or a related field; college or university teaching experience; three years teaching experience in elementary or secondary schools; administrative experience in teacher education; some experience with state agencies involved in teacher certification; and a dedication to excellence in higher education.

Desired Qualifications:
An appreciation for, and ability to

work with, faculty of divergent interests and styles; an ability to
interface in a positive and creative
manner with the public schools and
superior teaching abilities at both the
undergraduate and graduate classes.

Location: Southwestern United States
Type: College
Rating: 3-

Example 3.

Position: Dean, College of Education

Qualifications:
Applicants should have 1) a demonstrated commitment to fostering excellence
in research, teaching, and service; 2)
demonstrated skill as an academic
administrator; 3) a distinguished
scholarly record; 4) eligibility to
hold a full professorship in one of the
departments of the College.

Location: Eastern Shore United States
Type: University
Rating: 2-

Example 4.

Position: Dean, College of Education

Qualifications:
Requirements include an earned doctorate in education or a related field
and the ability to meet standards for
appointment as a tenured professor
within the college. Preference will be
given to candidates with: a record of
outstanding performance as an administrator; a record of leadership accomplishments in the educational community
and a role of educational advocacy;
evidence of commitment to the development of graduate programs in education;

a record of research and publication of
distinction; demonstrated commitment to
principles of affirmative action and
equal opportunity; knowledge regarding
allocations of financial resources and
budgetary matters; and previous
teaching experience.

Location: Midwest United States
Type: University
Rating: 3+

Example 5.

Position: Dean of the College of Education

Qualifications:

Qualifications sought include an earned
doctorate degree, a distinguished
academic record in teaching and in
research, and the ability to lead the
College in its academic responsibility
as part of a nationally and inter-
nationally recognized land grant
university.

Location: Midwest
Type: University
Rating: 2-

It is possible that applicants were provided with
additional qualifications upon request which could have
required public school experience as a teacher and
administrator.   Nevertheless, the vacancy notices
listed above say very little about requiring "front
line" public school experience except for Example 2 and
then only under "Desired Qualifications."

Colleges and schools of education are similar to
school districts when it comes to performance standards.   Too many of our training institutions are not
producing a quality product.   The leadership is weak
and many of the faculties are out of touch with the
real world of public education.   Deans and respective
faculties in our schools and colleges of education are
too often selected solely on the basis of scholarly

endeavors or political connections and not on teaching and administrative experiences in our public schools.

Would a hospital advertise for the position of chief of surgery without stating primary requirement, "experience in general surgery?" Would a company advertise for the position of programmer/analyst without stating primary requirement, "experience in systems analysis/programming?" Would a university advertise for the position of president without stating primary requirements, "experience in fund raising, fiscal management, administrative experience, and good communication skills?" Pick up the <u>Wall Street Journal</u>, turn to the classified section, and read the qualifications for top leadership positions in corporations. Proven management qualities and experience are required to make the first round cut.

The position of Dean, School/College of Education, must be held by an individual with outstanding leadership and management skills. Persons assuming this position should have, at one time or another, acquired experience in the public school sector both as a teacher and administrator. This experience should have included work in administrative areas of personnel, staff development, curriculum and instruction, and human relations. The Dean of the School/College of Education heads up the training program for future teachers and administrators, and the position carries the responsibility for advancing education within the state and throughout the country.

In Chapter 3 the need and importance of having strong leadership at the top of any organization was addressed. Schools of education are no exception. Too many deans and faculty members within schools of education tend to operate from ivory towers and fail to keep up with the changes and developments taking place in our public schools. The following questions should be asked each person applying for any school management position:

(1)   Why did you apply for the position?
(2)   What is your dominant, as well as supportive, management style? (Describe your style of management.)

(3)   How would you prefer to evaluate the performance of your staff members? How would you go about removing the "deadwood"?

(4)   Cite several major accomplishments you are proud of and were involved with at the public school level.

(5)   Share with us your failures and how you handled negative situations.

(6)   How good an administrator are you? Give reasons to support your claims.

(7)   Rank these areas according to priority as you would view them if you were chosen as Dean, School of Education:
a.   Publish - Research
b.   Teaching performance
c.   Working with school districts
d.   Long range planning
e.   Salary

The above format of questions are offered to illustrate the importance of selecting key management personnel in our colleges and schools of education who can lead an organization towards achieving its goals and who also understands public school operations.

Next, let's review a few samples of vacancy notices for teaching positions in higher education appearing also in 1984 issues of the Chronicle of Higher Education. The same rating scale of 1 = low to 5 = high will be used:

Example 1.

Position: Educational Administration
Assistant/Associate Professor

Qualifications:
Earned doctorate in educational administration: secondary school teaching experience; and public school administrative experience. Research and service activities will be considered.

Location: South

                        Type: University
                        Rating: 5-

Example 2.

    Position: Educational Administration
                 Assistant/Associate Professor

    Qualifications:
                 Qualifications include Ed.D. or Ph.D.
                 in educational administration and
                 recent public school administrative
                 experience, preferably as superin-
                 tendent or assistant superintendent.
                 Experience teaching at college or
                 university level and a record of
                 publication/research desirable.

                 Location: South
                 Type: University
                 Rating: 5+

Example 3.

    Position: Director of Student Teaching and Field
                 Experiences

    Qualifications:
                 Doctorate preferred with recent school
                 experience at the elementary education
                 level. Experience in the reading and
                 language arts areas.

                 Location: Midwest
                 Type: College
                 Rating: 4+

Example 4.

    Position: Assistant Professor, Elementary
                 Education

    Qualifications:
                 Earned doctorate and at least three
                 years public school teaching experience
                 required.

"Students respect teachers
who know how to teach
and are consistent in
doing so."

Location: Southeast
Type: College
Rating: 4+

The above vacancies for teaching positions at the university and college levels specifically require varying degrees of public school experience while previous management positions (Dean of School of Education) put little if any emphasis on public school experience. I can assure you, this situation has not recently changed.

Staffing our colleges and schools of education with administrators and professors who lack the vital experience of "front line" public school administration and teaching explains why so many of our education courses at our colleges and universities are viewed by the students as a waste of time. It is essential that deans of colleges and schools of education make the choice not only to maintain a continuing link with happenings in public schools themselves, but require their faculty members to get into the public schools and join up with administrators and teachers on a continuing basis, working together in research, instructional technology and training. I guarantee that such a requirement would lift the image of many of our campus education courses to a new height of respectability.

I recall reading of a well-known dean of a school of education from a Southern university speaking to a gathering of educators attending a meeting of the International Council on Education for Teaching and the American Association of Colleges for Teacher Education in Washington, D. C. In the December 1981 issue of Education Week, the dean blamed educators who prepare people for teaching for the lack of interest students are showing in international affairs and foreign languages. I am sure the dean was sincere in his remarks. However, we must first concentrate on the generic skills that lend themselves to the development of adequately prepared teachers and school administrators. Educational training institutions must produce a qualified product--qualified to teach and administrate effectively in our rural, suburban and urban public schools in this country. Professors of education must

then model effective teaching skills, regardless of
their areas of expertise.

I submit to the reader a challenge. Do as I did
several years ago when conducting a workshop at a university located in the East. Since I had some extra
time, I located the dean of education's office and
asked if it would be possible to observe an education
class. The dean suggested I go to observe a course
called "School Foundations." As I approached Room 205,
I noticed the professor bent over the podium with his
lecture notes before him. I gave him my visitor's
permission slip, and he suggested I take a seat in the
back of the room. The first thing that drew my attention was that three of the students who were sleeping
never woke up when I walked back to my seat. The
second thing I noticed was that two students on my
right were reviewing their educational psychology
notes. Third, I noticed several students were simply
staring out the window. Incidentally, there were
twelve students in the class. Finally, I observed the
monotone voice of the professor as he read from his
notes verbatim. Some thirty minutes later, the class
came to an end with the bell sounding which woke up the
three students who had slept through the class. The
other two students who were reviewing their educational
psychology notes closed their notebooks and, with the
window-staring students, made an exit for the door.
The professor's final words were "That's all for
today," and the class was dismissed. I thanked him for
the opportunity to visit his class and wished him well.

As I walked down the hall I thought to myself, "I
wonder how many times this scene is repeated throughout
our education schools in this country?" Needless to
say, I believe that anyone who teaches, regardless of
grade level, should strive to be the best in their
subject area. This is especially true of education
professors. I have heard it said many times over that
teachers who fail do so not because of a lack of knowledge but because they simply can't teach. In other
words, they lack an effective delivery system. Professors and teachers in our schools of education should
be models for effective, innovative, enthusiastic, and
stimulating methods of teaching.

Schools of education should be the "lighthouse" in displaying professors who can <u>teach</u> effectively. All too often the opposite is true. It is no secret that some of the poorest teaching occurs in our colleges and universities and, all too often, in schools of education. At many of our large universities, the emphasis is on "publish or perish" rather than on accountable teaching performance. The major requirement for college teaching is simply: The applicant "must be able to teach effectively." What makes for a successful teacher in our elementary and secondary schools equally applies to professors in education schools as well as throughout the university. Education professors especially should demonstrate what performance-base teaching is all about. But those associated with education schools know this is not the case. Requiring publication is a fine and noble demand, but many professors crank out "how to" and "solutions to" articles who are out of touch with today's public education or who lack public education experience. Such writings have little impact upon the readers in the field. It doesn't take much time for a veteran practitioner of teaching or administration to discover the solid professors vs. the weak ones. They can usually tell by the way they write and what they say whether or not they know what's happening in the real world.

The choice must be made that effective teaching should be the major criteria on which all higher education personnel are promoted and granted tenure. Publication and research are ample requirements but should not supersede teaching as a criteria for advancement in higher education, especially in our education schools.

Colleges and schools of education need to clean house on a consistent basis removing "deadwood" personnel and replacing vacant positions with accountable instructors who are familiar with the world of public education and who can teach effectively and serve as a model and mentor for students about to enter the world of modern-day public education. The "trainers" must possess the knowledge and expertise to train the trainees. No one wants a doctor operating on them who is not up to date with the techniques and "know how" of modern medicine. For example, there are approximately

150 students that enter a secondary teacher's classroom
each day, all with unique individual learning traits
and potential, not to mention individual behavior
patterns and multi-cultural backgrounds. A teacher
must be trained to handle such an assignment. Many of
our colleges and schools of education do not adequately
prepare teachers for this real world of frontline
teaching. Our graduates may know "what," but they
aren't trained in the "how." Ask any recent graduating
elementary or secondary teacher if they were adequately
trained to cope with the students of today's classrooms, and many will reply in the negative.

Knowing that graduate and undergraduate schools of
education were certifying and graduating student
teachers who couldn't teach, I outlined a plan for
school districts titled "Selecting First-Year Teachers"
which appeared in the 1977 February issue of the
National Association of Secondary School Principals
Bulletin. The plan was used in the Upper Darby School
District in Pennsylvania. It's no secret that taking
prescribed courses to acquire state teaching certification does not assure that an individual can teach.
All it does is validate to state officials that a
person has taken a list of prescribed courses and,
therefore, can be granted a teaching certificate in
that state. I contended in the article that student
teaching reports are often vague and highly subjective,
and it is difficult at best to correlate a grade point
average with actual teaching performance. I also
maintain that the standard interviewing process does
not always provide sufficient information to judge
teaching competencies. During interviewing sessions,
some candidates disguise their weaknesses effectively
by responding to all questions in a positive manner.
All of us have, on occasion, hired teachers who had
outstanding student-teaching recommendations and presented themselves well during the interview but ended
up as a teacher casualty after one semester.

The plan I then proposed consisted of the following steps:

Step 1. A number of applicants are initially
selected and interviewed by the personnel director of
the school district.

Step 2. The personnel director selects from four to six candidates that he feels are qualified and invites each one back for an interview with a committee comprised of the principal and several teachers from the building where the vacancy exists.

Step 3. Following the second interview, each committee member rates each candidate in the following areas: initiative, compatibility, knowledge, personality.

Step 4. Each of the final candidates completes a teacher inventory form which attempts to indicate whether the person favors a student-centered or teacher-centered approach to learning.

Step 5. Each of the final candidates is invited to teach a 10-minute mini-lesson videotaped to a group of five or six students. (The lesson topic would relate to the particular grade level where the vacancy exists.)

Step 6. Each committee member then analyzes the video tape performance of each candidate along with other data.

Step 7. Each committee member will then vote for the candidate he feels would best be able to assume the responsibilities and duties of the position.

Step 8. All votes are turned over to the personnel director and the candidate receiving the largest number of votes is recommended to the board of education. (In case of a tie, the credentials and data are re-evaluated, the building committee votes again.)

The program was an attempt to improve teacher-selection procedures with emphasis on performance. Now compare the above selection process with what goes on in the medical field. When a clinic, hospital, etc. recruits doctors, they seek out the best, based on medical training and performance. The necessary data to judge performance and qualifications is at hand, including extensive reports dealing with the competencies of the sought-after doctor. Once hired, hospitals don't send their newly-hired doctors to the operating

"Our people can't be
properly trained unless
they are first adequately
educated ... We are
running out of time
and no less than
the future of the
nation is at stake."

--James Burke, Chairman
Strategic Planning
Committee,
Johnson & Johnson

room to see if they can operate. Instead the doctors have been through the operating room while in medical school; and their performance, be it a specialty or otherwise, has been recorded, documented, and passed on to future employers and employment decisions can be made based on this performance. Should we expect any less from our education schools? Certification of teachers and administrators should guarantee above-average performance, but everyone in the education field knows that this is not so. It is not an uncommon practice to find teachers diagnosing a student's learning needs based on intuition and guesswork simply because they were never given the skills and knowledge base to do otherwise. The primary responsibility for turning out qualified teachers and administrators is with the colleges and universities. They must work jointly with state departments of education to assure school districts that their graduates in elementary and secondary education, as well as in administration, are qualified to teach and teach underlineeffectively and to administrate and administrate underlineeffectively. This is a tall order for many state departments of education and colleges/schools of education because to follow a training program of accountability will mean a complete revamping of standards, requirements, personnel and planning.

I am of the belief, based on administrative and teaching experience at the school district and university levels, that current federal and state reform packages aimed at providing excellence in education will have difficulty in obtaining desired outcomes until there is a major overhaul of the way we train teachers and administrators. There should be fierce competition among graduate and undergraduate schools of education to see who can turn out a better "product." But present conditions clearly reveal that many of our teacher and administration training programs lack accountability.

The stockholders of public education (local taxpayers) are finding it difficult to support tax increases for higher teacher salaries when the standard of performance is average or below par.

In addition, graduate schools of education must

make the choice to clear up the confusion over research and teaching. This author takes the position of supporting research study in our schools of education and considers it a vital ingredient in the training of educators. However, this is not to suggest that faculties of education schools should involve their students with theory and research work that has little if any practical application to performing successfully in the field. I take the position that the real benefits and prestige for schools of education can come when the choice is made within each college to create a separate team of competent faculty members who spend the majority of their time and study doing research. Such professionals may not be the greatest motivators in the eyes of the students, but they are deep thinkers, with analytical minds which makes them competent researchers. This idea would parallel the practices used in major corporations where there is a separate research and development division. With schools of education having their own research division or department, students would be exposed to findings and conclusions involving basic and applied research in teaching and administration as a required component of their training program. The "think tank" department would work closely with practitioners in the field, probing deeper into such areas as student learning modalities, generic and personality skills associated with effective administration and teaching, staff evaluation techniques, human dynamics, and curriculum development.

Research in education has long been the hallmark of prestige for colleges. In the most up-to-date study (1983) by Maurice Eash, professor of urban education research at the University of Illinois at Chicago, a list of 25 institutions (colleges and universities) that produced the most education-related research between 1975 and 1981 was given.

1. Stanford University, California
2. University of California, Los Angeles
3. University of Illinois, Urbana-Champaign
4. University of Wisconsin, Madison
5. University of California, Berkeley
6. University of Illinois, Chicago
7. University of Minnesota

8. Harvard University, Massachusetts
9. Pennsylvania State University
10. Ohio State University
11. University of California, Santa Barbara
12. Johns Hopkins University, Maryland
13. Indiana University
14. University of Michigan
15. University of Texas, Austin
16. University of Pittsburg, Pennsylvania
17. Purdue University, Indiana
18. University of Chicago, Illinois
19. University of Southern California
20. Northwestern University, Illinois
21. University of North Carolina, Chapel Hill
22. Columbia University, New York
23. Cornell University, New York
24. Michigan State University
25. Rutgers University, New Jersey

Continued emphasis should be placed on research studies relating to the improvement of instruction, student discipline, teacher effectiveness, professional training, and behavior modification. Over the years, various studies have been conducted in these areas, but more needs to be done.

The choice to be persistent must accompany the research. Opening up one door will open another and another until someday there will be a major break-through in areas that could revolutionize education and teaching beyond our present predictions. Again looking at the medical field, one finds constant ongoing research taking place in universities and hospitals throughout the world, aimed at making human beings healthier and better able to combat diseases. The research in cancer and heart disease is a good example. Research by the medical profession in these two areas has been practical. Philosophies won't cure. Now patients afflicted by these dreaded diseases are better able to overcome their illnesses, and in increasing instances, be cured completely.

Accountable research work is needed in education. The challenge facing many schools of education is to hire faculty members who are competent researchers and who, at the same time, understand the real world of public education.

Much of the research work done currently in our schools of education is tied into doctoral studies and dissertations. Deans' Network, a national organization of deans from schools and colleges of education that grant doctoral degrees, appointed a five-member research team to survey some thirty-seven deans whose institutions of higher learning granted Ed.D. or Ph.D. degrees in education. From their study, the team quoted some of the more interesting responses in the May 1984 <u>Phi Delta Kappan</u>.

One dean stated, "What I think is so important is that we finally realize that, for a professional school, formal knowledge, as well as practical knowledge, is important. A large part of what schools of education should be about is figuring out how to integrate formal knowing and practical knowing...with a respect for both."

Another group of deans took a more practical approach in responding. As one dean in this group responded:

> Superintendents who come here to get
> their doctorates are not necessarily
> interested in becoming scholars but
> rather topflight practitioners. Some of
> our counseling psychology students want
> to go into private practice - not to
> create new knowledge or to teach or to
> do research. In a way, all research/-
> scholar programs are a little schizo-
> phrenic.

The study team reported that their sample revealed many deans followed the policies formulated by faculty groups as stated in the following response:

> Another factor that significantly
> affects the role of deans is the amount
> of autonomy enjoyed by departments or
> other units that offer degree programs.
> Some schools of education have long
> traditions of faculty governance; here

the dean's primary role is to administer
policies established by faculty groups.
Most of the institutions in our sample
fall into this category and many of the
deans are not only comfortable with this
situation but would prefer it no other
way.

A recent poll conducted by The Executive Educator,
(1988) of superintendents and principals revealed that
the majority of those responding stated they received
"poor" or "fair" training in major school operations
while attending graduate school. Less than twenty-five
percent reported that a professor "had a significant
impact on their career development." "Too many
professors have never worked in a public school" was
the summary of the written responses.

I submit the following thought to those readers
who have attended some institution of higher learning.
List those professors whom you admired and respected
for their effective teaching and training. Next,
compare this number to the total number of professors
you had and figure out the percentage. I dare say your
percentage of "good teachers" is low. I would seriously propose that this analysis be done by all of those
who have graduated and received a teaching or administrative certificate as well as a degree from a
college or school of education. One would assume the
percentage would be higher, but I would venture to say
the percentage of "good professors" would be something
we would not want to publicize.

At the University of Kansas back in 1979, a group
of education professors representing all departments in
the school of education came together to map out a plan
of action for the future. The emphasis was on pre-
paring effective beginning teachers. Incorporating
support from an advisory group made up of superintendents, teacher union presidents, representatives of the
state department of education, state school board
members, and state board of education representatives,
a teacher-training program was offered which revealed a
five-year comprehensive training program. Students
were to earn 132 semester hours by the end of their
senior year and have a grade point average of 3.0 in

"Professors of education
should be the models of
what good teaching
is all about."

order to advance to the fifth year. The fifth year was divided into three parts: student teaching (first half of fall semester), practicum in the schools (final two-thirds of the second semester), and a period of graduate level course work. Undergraduate studies include 1) growth and development of children, 2) interpersonal communications and self-concept, 3) research measurement and technology.

Similar five-year programs have been underway at an increasing number of colleges and universities recently which include the following features:

- establishment of solid criteria to determine if a student is qualified to teach;
- more emphasis on clinical and field work;
- involving public school personnel in program and certification development;
- the addition of the fifth year of study; and
- course offerings that are relevant in today's world of public education.

Teacher preparation programs must change. First, they must change their programs in order to keep up with the times of modern-day public education; and second, colleges and schools of education must improve the quality of teaching within their own ranks through accountable evaluation methods and offering salaries to the "producers" comparable to those in the field. When these two goals are undertaken, the case for requesting additional funding in order to guarantee decent and competitive salaries for college faculty members can be substantiated. Remember, when the product improves, the public is more willing to invest their money. When youngsters come home from school telling their parents what an exciting and wonderful day they had at school and relating what a good teacher Mrs. Jones is, the parents are more apt to become supportive of their schools.

Teachers must be trained and trained properly. Administrators must be trained and trained properly. Leadership starts at the top, beginning with our schools of education. A dean of a college of education within a university setting is like a school superintendent; he must be a manager and a leader who is not afraid to make decisions and stand behind those convictions that are aimed at improving the quality of training and performance of the graduates and faculty.

I applauded Dr. John Silber, President of Boston University, when he said, "There are schools of education which, like Pontius Pilate, wash their hands of what goes on in schools. There is no place for innocence. We cannot stand by watching a disaster and refuse to help." Dr. Silber's comments were reported in the September 7, 1988, issue of Education Week, announcing that Boston University was in the process of taking over and managing the Chelsea School District, a city of 25,000 located across Mystic River from Boston. The faltering school system, on the decline during recent years, suffered from high unemployment, poor facilities, low tax base, declining test scores, and a rising non-English speaking student body which presently stood at 3,300. The present dean of the School of Education at Boston University served as the CEO of the project and the central office. The educational "profit - loss" statement of the Chelsea School District has raised a number of questions: Have test scores improved? Has student attendance increased? Has professional morale improved? Has adequate financing been made available? Has professional staff attendance improved? With evidence that there has been poor leadership at the school level, the proposed 10-year agreement will provide ample time to the new governing body to turn things around. The choice was made by a president of a major university to move out in front and put his school of education in a position of addressing the modern day challenges of public education in this country.

This marked the first time a university has taken over the operation of a public school system in this country. This was a move that put accountability on the line. Education schools in this country should be expected and capable of moving into any school system and doing the job necessary to achieve a vision of educational excellence. To state otherwise means simply the training and expertise is not up to par; and if such is the case, it might be in the best interest of the university as well as the taxpayers to close the doors on the educational school. A school of education, taking over the managing of a school system, forces professors into the schools and administrative offices where many have not been for years. Why should we expect anything less of our education schools when medical schools, dental schools, and law schools, for example, offer their direct services to the public on a daily basis. This is how to build accountability and recognition. Professors of education should be able to walk into any public school system in this country and "operate" effectively within the area of their expertise.

For years, higher education faculty members have been notorious for telling the public how bad our public schools are, yet they are the trainers of the teachers going into our public schools!

The National Commission on Excellence in Education was an eighteen-member panel appointed by previous Secretary of Education, Terrel H. Bell, to examine the American educational system with accompanying recommendations. Reporting on teacher-training programs, the following findings were disclosed in the September 1988 issue of Education Week.

> . Too many teachers are being drawn from the bottom quarter of graduating high school and college students.

> . The teacher preparation curriculum is weighted heavily with courses in "educational methods" at the expense of courses in subjects to be taught. A survey of 1,350 institutions training teachers indicated that 41 percent of the time of elementary school teacher candidates is spent in education courses, which reduces the amount of time available for subject matter courses.

It is a fact that college students who fail to make it in other fields switch to education in order to assure themselves a major field of concentration and a degree. According to the <u>Profile of SAT's and Achievement Test Taking,</u> the average Scholastic Aptitude Test scores for college-bound seniors in 1988 were 428 verbal and 476 math. Of those who planned to major in education, the average scores were 407 verbal and 442 math. Although scores don't always indicate who can teach and who can't, education schools can no longer continue to be the dumping ground for those students who fail to make it in other fields.

There are various social forces that cause the low quality of students entering education programs, such as the conditions that impact salaries and public support. But overriding these social factors is the lack of accountable and stimulating college and university schools of education.

With the decline in qualified students entering the teaching profession, enrollment in many of our education schools has also dropped. To combat the declining enrollment situation, some schools of education have lowered admission standards. Such a move will only compound the serious situation presently existing in our country's teacher training institutions.

Teacher candidates should know their subject matter and know it well. But they also must know how to effectively teach that subject matter. College and university method courses taught by competent professors, aware of the instructional methods and practices that go into the making of a good teacher, are equally important or, some would argue, more important than full knowledge of subject matter.

Competency tests for teachers are gaining wide acceptance by state legislators. The thrust for competency testing has come about because school districts were hiring teachers only to discover they were not competent in their field of concentration. A junior high math teacher who cannot do basic fractions doesn't belong in the classroom. Any teacher who lacks basic grammar skills does not belong in the classroom. Many of our colleges and schools of education are graduating elementary and secondary teacher candidates who have

"If you think education
is expensive,
try ignorance."

--Derek Bok, President
Harvard University

minimal writing and math skills.

Competency tests for teachers measure minimal basic knowledge but not teaching performance. Performance is not easily measured, but results of student achievement scores and how students perceive the teacher's instructional package must become a part of the total evaluation process when judging teacher performance.

Many of the present merit pay programs for teachers, another issue gaining much notoriety and stimulating controversy, will not necessarily improve teacher performance. Why? The merit pay proposals do not directly focus on teaching performance. Merit pay is determined by such things as assuming extra curricular duties and enrolling in additional education courses. These are secondary factors and, of and by themselves, will not improve teacher performance.

We come back to the same questions: Can the majority of our present-day teacher candidates teach and teach effectively? Are our schools of education turning out a qualified product?

Isabel Carpio was an outstanding elementary teacher prior to her retirement. I had the privilege of knowing Isabel when she taught remedial reading in Aurora, Illinois. She was truly an outstanding professional teacher. One day she came into my office and informed me of her intentions to retire. I knew her mind was made up, and I had little chance of talking her out of it. Any superintendent hates to lose a good teacher. I told Isabel how much the children, staff, and community would miss her; but if there was ever a person who earned their retirement and then some, it was Isabel Carpio. She was a lady of high principles and manners--a demanding teacher who brought out the best in each student. One day I picked up the newspaper and noticed in the Letter to the Editor section a letter with the title "A Toast for Educators." The letter follows:

Editor, The Beacon News:

At the end of every school year, tributes

are paid to the top educators, administrators
and scholars. I would like to propose a toast
of champagne to each and every teacher in both
the public and private sectors.

Into the hands of these teachers falls the
heavy task of educating the Youth, the hope of
our future. The teacher becomes an influential figure in the student's world for ten
months every year during the child's formative
and most impressionable stage of growth.

Teaching has been called the noblest, and
may I add, the most demanding profession. To
be successful, a teacher must learn to
superbly practice the art of super salesman-
ship - selling his service of educating,
selling the knowledge and skills he is
expected to impart and cultivate, selling the
ideals and mores that lead to a better quality
of life.

A good teacher has to be alert every
second of the working day - teaching the
cognitive basic skills, developing concepts
and creative thinking, ministering to the
individual physical and emotional needs of
some 25 to 30 students - while providing a
learning environment that is healthy and
enjoyable. A teacher who is not exhausted at
the end of the day must not have done a good
day's job.

Stressful situations are daily occurrences
in the classroom. Studies have shown that a
certain degree of stress challenges human
nature to greater heights and teachers use
this principle to stimulate learning. When a
teacher feels his work is just routine, then
dull mechanical lessons result.

Children quickly sense this. When students are so carefree as to be complacent,
then success or failure wouldn't mean much to
them.

Thus, it is the teacher's responsibility
to provide the balance that would bring out
realistic values. Every teacher is on his
toes in the classroom selling the art of
"learning" to minds that are often swamped
with TV programs, movies, video games and

entertainment from the competitive world of the commercial arts.

Some complain that teachers get too many "off" days. As one who had taught for 38 years, I do know that those breaks come at the most opportune times. Those vacations give much needed periods to recoup lagging physical and mental strengths; every come back from these break points affords newer, fresher outlooks and attitudes.

Do teachers really take a vacation from their work? Far from it! They go on trips to gather more information and insights to use in enriching the students' lives, to shop for more devices to use for next year or to meet other teachers from whom they can learn more techniques of good teaching. It is human nature to want to succeed. Teachers, especially, want and need to succeed in the tremendous responsibility entrusted unto them.

Here's to more patience and success in your undertaking.

Here's to your efforts and dedication for the school year about to end!

Isabel E. Carpio

The letter is offered to the reader because it says so much about what teaching is all about. Every college and university faculty member who has the responsibility of developing and training future teachers should strive to produce teachers like this lady. The choice for education schools must be to strive towards greater heights in order to produce teachers who are competent and qualified to teach in our public schools.

Qualified and competent teachers stand out among their peers. They stand out because they never quit growing professionally. Some claim good teachers are born with gifted talents to teach. Technically, I guess there is some truth in this, but I also know training plays a vital part in any profession--be it teaching, medicine, law, dentistry, etc. It must not be taken lightly. Excellence in education is a tre-

mendous goal to pursue. The achievement of such a goal
will be realized through improved teaching and effective administration in our public schools. Colleges and
schools of education must choose to graduate quality
products. Quality teachers will inspire and attract
young students to the profession. Once this occurs,
many doors will be open that can lead to solving critical issues in today's world of public education. In
the 150-year history of our teacher-training programs,
the expectations have never been greater. Failure to
address the current issue of training can lead to
serious consequences in our total public education
system. More than ever, we need top-notch teachers and
school administrators to lead and prepare our students
for the future so that this country will remain a
nation of achievement and growth.

Now is the time to act. Time will not permit any
more dragging of the feet in an attempt to improve our
teacher training institutions. Everyone must make the
choice to support plans for improving our education
schools--business people, community leaders, educators,
politicians--because everyone has an investment at
stake.

Chapter 6

Self-Interest Groups: How Powerful Are They?

"Thus, those skilled in conflict take the initiative over others so that others do not take the initiative."

--Sun Tzu
taken from
The Art of Strategy

Anyone involved in public education has been associated with groups of people who band together because of a common goal, situation, or concern. Groups of this nature have brought forth many positive changes in national, state, and local politics in this country as well as in public education. Persons in such groups as the Sierra Club, Mothers Against Drunk Drivers, A.A.R.P., and Handgun Control, Inc. have banded together to bring about changes in the environment, in legislation, and within our communities. The public may or may not agree with or support all these special interest groups; but whatever cause one wishes to champion, one can trust there will be a group to join dealing with that interest.

The need in public education is to organize groups of motivated people to bring about necessary changes even if those changes produce conflict. Constructive interest groups raise money for specific needs - from improving the physical plant (such as carpeting, computers or air conditioning) to financing band trips, hiring tutors, and calling school board and school administrator's attention to needs of the teachers and their students. Most schools depend heavily on the most helpful groups within the system - the parent organizations such as P.T.A., Band Boosters, or Room Parents. These groups of dedicated volunteers often make the difference between a mediocre school environment and an exciting school environment. These parents have the school's best interest at heart. They are publicly supportive and are enthusiastic volunteers. They care about their children's education and are willing to work or contribute to help teachers and school administrators. They work within the system to bring about needed change. They take time to become acquainted with the teachers and administrators.

Occasionally, a group will form that can cause frustration and chaos within a school system. If the author did not know from personal experience how prevalent and poisonous this kind of group situation is, this chapter would not be necessary. Unfortunately, there are many schools and school districts that are affected by negative individuals and groups who through insinuation, rumor, and negative public comments can undermine the efforts of the very persons who need and expect their support. There are schools with ineffective teachers and administrators, and they should be removed from their position. But there are approved methods of doing that. What I am referring to are those groups, usually small in number but powerful, that use mean-spirited tactics to undermine the efforts of teachers, principals, superintendents and/or school boards. Disgruntled parents, temporary problems, or negative situations which are misinterpreted by the public are experienced everywhere and are usually quickly handled. But there are groups of people who, in the midst of a problem, come together in order to gain control of decision, policy and personnel matters within their school district. I term these groups self-interest groups.

Over the years, much of the dissension and conflict infiltrating many of our public school systems has been perpetuated and promoted by such groups. School administrators, board of education members, mayors, corporations, college and university officials

have been subject to the wrath inflicted by these
groups, especially those groups who adhere to radical
methods. Joseph Rowson, a school administrator from
Nebraska, presented a summary of the more common
tactics used by modern-day subscribers of the Alinsky
methods in the March 1983 issue of The School Administrator. (Saul Alinsky, despite a deep concern for
people, was branded by many as a radical. A graduate
student in criminology at the University of Chicago in
the early 1920's, Alinsky focused his attention on the
black neighborhoods and their repression by the "establishment." Although his intent was altruistic, his
methods often involved incitement and hostility.)
Rowson summarized the Alinski tactics as follows:

. Packing meetings with members of the employee
  or citizen organization, disrupting the
  normal business of the governing body and
  forcibly and publicly demanding individual
  commitments from members of that body to
  support the group's demands.

. Developing confusing patterns of organization
  and leadership for the employee or citizen
  group making it difficult for those outside
  the group to know who is really in control.

. Publishing misleading or erroneous information about the governing body's members
  often using out-of-context quotes to point up
  how uncaring, paternalistic, and oppressive
  the establishment is towards its employees or
  its constituents.

. Launching telephone campaigns which feature
  numerous calls to each board or council
  member indicating he is "the only one who
  understands the situation" and that he must
  be a mediator to change the other members'
  direction.

. Making insulting statements to administrative
  officials, particularly the superintendent or
  the mayor, deliberately intended to make the
  official angry, and hoping that, in an
  emotional state, he will lack proper judgment

and make mistakes.

- Requesting marathon, round-the-clock sessions
  to resolve issues presented by the opposed
  group (for example, at the bargaining table
  in a teacher negotiation situation).

- Picketing administrative or governmental
  buildings for the specific sites where
  services are delivered (the individual
  schools in a district, for example).

- Using advertising campaigns which state the
  employee or citizen groups' grievances in the
  most dramatic way possible, pointing out the
  administrations or the governing body's
  paternalistic, ineffective handling of those
  grievances.

There are many public school officials who have
had personal experiences with groups using these
methods. Some local and state teachers' union organizations have been accused of subscribing to Alinsky
tactics from time to time, especially during collective
bargaining sessions. Whether the assertion is true or
not is debatable. However, those of us who have had
experience with teacher strikes can attest to the fact
that the disruptive tactics listed by Rowson do occur.

Teacher unions are not the only groups that have
been accused of using radical overthrow tactics aimed
at the "school establishment." Technically, when more
than one person aligns himself with another person or
others on a controversial issue, they can be classified
as a special group. We have seen committees that use
the name "Parents for Better Schools," or "Committee on
Progressive Education," or "Committee to Save Our
Schools" that had their origin with one or two angry
people. It doesn't always take a major episode in a
school district to invite negative reaction. In many
cases it's the little things that can cause trouble.
It is relatively simple to develop an issue against the
administration or the school board and carry an issue
to the extreme. For example, a seemingly simple issue,
and one that can inflame some individuals and can cause
self-interest groups to rise up out of the ground over-

night, is the last-minute closing of schools due either to inclement weather or heating and water problems. School administrators, especially superintendents, constantly run the risk of upsetting parents when schools are closed unexpectedly for whatever reason. With more parents working, a change in school plans for the day can cause problems among the working fathers and mothers, especially if their young sons and daughters require adult supervision. Instead of accepting the obvious need to close schools on occasion, upset parents can feed on each other's anger, then band together to attack the school district.

In Chapter 1, I listed a sample of topics and issues that came before boards of education during my years as a school administrator that were initiated and fueled by self-interest groups. Many of these topics and issues were of minor significance; but I can assure you, they became highly controversial before the smoke cleared. Innocent people became victims of vindictiveness and ridicule.

Public schools have been bombarded with statements and charges as to what should and should not have been done. Groups of people then have joined together to voice their opinions at school board meetings. Out of these bands of people, other controversial problems arise and the beginning of another self-interest group is formed. Many of these groups appear before the board before they avail themselves of the facts. I have observed board of education meetings consisting of three-fourths non-agenda comments and one-fourth agenda items. These situations can create a backlog in decision-making on critical issues, which promotes administrative staff and school board "meeting burnout." Under these conditions, the question must be asked, "Who is in charge of the school district - the board of education and the superintendent or the self-interest groups?" "Change is needed and we are the only ones who can save our school systems from disaster" is often heard from self-interest groups. That may be true. I'm not arguing against change; I'm arguing against underhanded methods to achieve change.

As I noted in Chapter 1, legitimate concerns and issues need to be brought to the attention of the board

of education and the superintendent. Constructive
input should be sought after constantly. Parents and
the community-at-large need to know what is happening
in their schools; and they have a right, as a taxpayer
and parent, to voice their opinions over issues that
have a direct relationship to the welfare and future of
the education of their children. Parents and interested citizens should be kept informed of school district
happenings and should be encouraged by school administrators to serve on curriculum committees, parent-
teacher organizations, long-range planning committees,
etc. Board of education meetings need to have an
agenda item indicating "Audience Request to Speak"
where, with time limits, opportunity is granted to
address the board. But at the same time, decisive
action must be taken by the board of education, especially the president, to prevent turmoil and ineffi-
ciency within the school district caused by radical
self-interest groups who march to the tune of the
Alinsky Plan of Radicalism. Progress does not occur
within any organization when there is chaos and dissension created by radical forces from the outside.

One of the primary ways to prevent radical self-
interest group takeover in a school district is to
maintain strong team leadership at the top, starting
with the board of education. The citizens and staff
need to observe "take charge" management. There is
nothing more reassuring to the total staff of any
school district then to have a board of education who
will not tolerate attempts by radical groups to take
over the school district. When the opposite is true,
interest groups gain control of the school district
operations by informing individual board of education
members how to vote, some even scheduling their own
separate, private meetings. When this occurs, a school
district begins to come apart at the top management
level. The school system then becomes vulnerable to
open criticism and ridicule by the press and taxpayers.
When self-interest groups gain a foothold in the district, the foothold can last seemingly forever with the
results being extremely destructive. Superintendents
are fired; teacher uprisings occur; staff morale and
instructional advancement decline; and the children,
the most important commodity of the school district,
suffer. The educational environment deteriorates

"Today's world of
public education is
not as bad as many
think, if the public
would only take a
look inside."

because the emphasis on good teaching and good instruction is undermined when the district is under fire.
With a struggle for power among groups, combined with
feuding, jealousy and "what's the use" feelings,
teaching becomes a chore rather than a delight.   In
such a negative working environment, personnel jump
ship.   Good, dedicated board members do not seek re-
election.   Pride in the school district begins to erode
while the self-interest groups continue to place emphasis on their own pet projects rather than supporting
the goals already established.

A lot of red tape could be reduced if the process
of deciding critical issues in our public schools were
to become more streamlined and not left to self-
interest groups.   When policies are set and strongly
upheld, many issues will not need to be dealt with
interminably - the policies are already in place.   This
is the advantage of early parent involvement.   Interested parents can help formulate policies and because
of their vested interest, help support these goals.

If a school district bows to the pressures of
selfish groups, especially those with radical goals,
the question becomes, "Why employ a superintendent?"
If decision making is handled by radical groups, it is
hard to justify the employment of a chief school
executive or any other school officials.

Let me offer some effective guidelines to follow
in dealing with radical self-interest groups.   The list
is not intended to be the answer to handling all controversy arriving from public school issues, but it
will serve to reduce friction and tension between
school officials and the public.

> . Boards of education should establish a
>   written policy regarding procedures and
>   guidelines for responding to questions from
>   the public.
> . Board of education meetings should be
>   conducted in a professional manner adhering
>   to Roberts Rules of Order and following an
>   agenda published and available prior to
>   meetings.
> . Board of education presidents should exert

leadership and foresight and fully understand management boundaries as they relate to the board of education and the superintendent in dealing with the public.
. School board members should not have separate private board meetings. Private meetings, without public notice, are illegal in most states.
. Board of education members should not individually make promises and convey confidential information to individuals and groups within the community.
. An ongoing network of communications should be established by the administration in the school district that reaches out to the public for input as well as conveying school happenings and events.
. The administration should extend an invitation to key community and business leaders to tour the school district. Board members should conduct the tour.
. At all times board of education members and the administration should refrain from emotional outbursts and sarcasm when responding to public questions.
. Board of education members and the administration, especially the superintendent, should do their homework prior to each public meeting including anticipating questions that might be asked by members of the public.

The choice should be made by school boards and the administration to follow the above guidelines in addressing radical self-interest groups. Such efforts will serve to enhance teamwork between the board of education and the administration and will create a more positive image to the public especially during controversial times.

A major controversial issue that usually generates self-interest groups in this country involves the teaching of religion and moral values in the schools. Some states, especially those in the Midwest (Iowa, Oklahoma, Nebraska, Kansas), have seen certain parents remove their children from the public school systems and enroll them in church-operated schools or home schools which are not state certified. This action often causes serious community division. There are documented cases that individuals have been jailed and that law enforcement agencies have placed padlocks on church and school doors. State education officials claim such schools do not follow state required standards relating to course requirements, certified teachers, safety standards, length of school day, and health regulations.

Home instruction is offered by parents who have refused to send their children to the public schools and instead, for various reasons, elected to educate them at home. Some claim public schools have an environment causing the decay of the spiritual and moral values of their children. Some feel they can better prepare their children academically at home. This author believes parents should have the option of providing home instruction to their children if they can provide sufficient evidence that state standards can be met. However, for a variety of reasons, I would not personally make that choice. In my opinion, children need a quality education within a pluralistic social setting. The strife and conflict caused by radical self-interest groups regarding home instruction have caused certain common interest parents to become discouraged and frustrated with public education. As controversial as the issue has become, the results of home instruction can be interesting.

Several years ago, a case came up in California where an 18-year-old was educated by his parents on a remote ranch. The youth then took the Scholastic Aptitude Test. The results of the test revealed a score in the top five percent of high school seniors who took the test. Upon review of the application, Harvard University officials admitted the boy as one of the 2200 new students entering in the fall of 1983. The youth did have some previous college classroom experience. Records show that he took some advance course work (18 hours) at a junior college the year before and earned a perfect "A" average. The parents of the boy were college graduates--his mother a former high school English teacher and his father a college professor (<u>Education Week</u>, September 1983).

There are many examples of people with self-interest ideas making choices in opposition to mainstream theories but doing so quietly and effectively without negatively forcing their opinions and judgements on the rest of the school district.

The majority of home instruction cases do not always turn out happily. Even with some of the unsettling things we hear about public education these days, there is only one choice that can be made by parents in gaining an acceptable <u>overall</u> education for their children and that is through attending an accountable certified accredited school or school system. In addition, there are the side benefits of developing and acquiring skills involved in dialogue and team play and in learning how to handle opposing points of view.

Self-interest groups of a radical nature can appear anywhere within a school system. Probably no area receives more public attention than in the world of school sports. Disgruntled groups of alumni fans ban together to "fire the coach" or call for mass boycott of attendance. They may illegally subsidize those activities in which they have a vested interest. When Texas voted in the "no pass - no play" rule, groups of parents wrote hate mail to the governor's special committee which was formed to upgrade the level of education in that state. With such tactics, one begins to question which is more important to the public - getting a good education or having a winning football season?

The goal of education is to train a child to become literate in order to function in society as a lifelong learner. Learning to read, write, and compute are the desired outcomes of education. Schools without leadership and controlled by self-interest groups cannot attain these objectives.

The existing conditions in our society influence happenings in our schools. With an increasing divorce rate, job stress and transient life styles in this country, many parents, as well as students, take their personal insecurities and frustrations out on the schools. They do so by banding together to vent their frustrations and anger. Boards of education and school officials are usually the recipients of such behavior. For such individuals, self-interest groups serve as an emotional escape valve. Group dynamics play an important part in making such people feel liked and wanted. Before an individual involves or aligns himself with any cause, certain questions must be asked: "What is my motivation for becoming a part of this?" "Do I really know all the facts?" "Is it fair?" To complicate matters, we find various members of a board of education joining the forces of such groups from time to time. This can become a real nightmare for any superintendent of schools. For example, take the issue of confidentiality. Correspondence from the superintendent's office addressed to members of the board of education and marked confidential is soon discovered to be public information. Members of self-interest groups know the contents of the correspondence as soon as it arrives in the hands of board members. Superintendents caught in this situation may continue to send out confidential information knowing quite well that no longer is anything confidential in the school district. Such a development destroys the teamwork practices of the management in the school district. Members of a board of education who let themselves fall into this trap are not only hurting themselves, but they are also hurting the school district since they are no longer acting on behalf of the total citizenry but instead on behalf of the radical few who want to control the school system. One superintendent told me recently, "I have two suitcases, one is always packed; when the board of education starts to routinely split votes then I start packing the other, because the end is in sight."

Groups who use negative radical methods to gain control of a school district's operations usually aim their shots first at the superintendent, hoping to knock him out through forced resignation or by creating pressure to keep the contract from being renewed. After the superintendent is taken care of, their next target is usually certain members of the board of education (those who fail to align themselves with the group's cause) or other administrators, usually at the principalship level. Such groups can verbally attack parents and citizens who fail to support their cause.

I have seen innocent people get caught up in the turmoil and conflict of the power struggle. Name calling,
slander, social pressure, personal property damage, and
physical violence have characterized many struggles
within school districts.

Those experienced in the various strategies of
group dynamics and behavior know the importance of
getting the media involved in controversial issues.
Naturally, the news media always has and will continue
to enjoy controversy, especially when it occurs at
public meetings. Coverage of "rip snorting" public
gatherings such as those that occur at public school
board meetings across this country sells newspapers and
television time. Media coverage can be constructive as
well as destructive, depending on the intensity of the
issues. Gaining control of the media is a primary goal
of radical self-interest groups in school districts
throughout our country. Incidents that "get out of
hand" at public school board meetings draw media attention. Clues that indicate this is happening, according
to a joint 1984 report prepared by the American Association of School Administrators and National School
Boards Association entitled Holding Effective Board
Meetings, are easy to identify:

- A person with a complaint talking beyond a
  time limit, repeating what already has been
  said.
- Members of the audience commenting from their
  chairs without being recognized and
  identifying themselves.
- Members of the audience talking to each other
  or debating board members instead of
  addressing all comments to the board
  chairman.

As the joint report stated, a firm policy is needed as well as a chairperson who is in control. A
policy, according to the report, should "welcome the
public, invite participation, and clarify rules for
that participation." These rules might include some or
all of the following:

- At a particular point in the agenda,
  recognize the public.

"A true colleague
is one who
supports you
behind your back."

. Require would-be speakers to sign in at the door.
. Suggest that the board refer all items of an administrative nature to the superintendent rather than hear them at the meeting.
. Set limits for each speaker.
. Address all comments to the board chairman.

According to the National School Boards Association, people come to school board meetings "because they have a personal interest in the agenda item, the controversy surrounding an item intrigues them, and because they believe real school decisions are made in meetings."

The NSBA research (Holding Effective Board Meetings, 1984) continues by suggesting that "individuals concerned about one agenda item might try to engineer a sufficiently large attendance to convince the board that the entire community is interested in their cause." Board members must realize that a room full of people does not necessarily represent the "will of the community" or good education for all students.

According to the joint report of the NSBA (National School Boards Association) and AASA (American Association of School Administrators) from a sample of school leaders from across the country, school leaders report that public controversy should be anticipated when these items are on the agenda:

. Closing, redistricting or desegregating schools;
. Introducing courses on human sexuality or ethics;
. Cutting programs - especially if teachers, but not administrators, lose jobs;
. Cutting staff, settling strikes, or shifting staff among schools; or
. Raising local taxes.

Not only are the above topics controversial, but they demand a great deal of meeting time to resolve. An effective leader who is in charge of a meeting will speed the decision-making process along by preventing lengthy and unnecessary discussion. It requires a

"take charge" person to accomplish this task, usually
the responsibility of the president of the board of
education or the superintendent.

Board meetings can take up too much time unless
certain procedures are followed. Drawing upon my own
experiences as well as suggestions from Holding Effective Board Meetings, a plan like the one offered below
is needed and must be followed in order to reduce the
length of meetings and to offer ways to reduce anticipated or unexpected audience disruptions.

Example 1.

>   Situation

1. Members arrive late,
    too much outside con-
    versation while meeting
    is in progress.

    Board should have
    coffee, etc.
    available one-half
    hour before meeting
    to give opportunity
    for greetings, visit-
    ing, and communicat-
    ing. The gavel must
    be sounded precisely
    at the appointed hour
    regardless of who is
    not present.

2. Members do not stick
    to issues, repeat
    hearsay, dominate
    discussions.

    The agenda must be
    distributed to each
    board of education
    member several days
    prior to the meeting
    incorporating the
    following headings:
    Items for Discussion,
    Items for Informa-
    tion, and Items Re-
    quiring Decisions.
    All who wish to speak
    to an item must indi-
    cate ahead of time
    and a fair time limit
    must be enforced for
    each speaker. Copies

of agenda should be available to the public ahead of meeting time. Agenda topics should be reported to the media.

3. There is a lack of organization, order or understanding of issues.

The superintendent and president must go over the agenda together, item by item, prior to meeting to make certain each issue is fully understood. The president must see to it board members "do their homework" prior to meetings.

4. The meeting is lengthened by routine matters such as approving purchase orders and reading meetings.

The president moves that all routine items be acted upon together.
The superintendent uses consent agenda.

5. There are non-agenda items introduced by board members or audience at meeting.

The president asks board members if they believe the item is (1) in the board's domain, or (2) urgent enough to warrant discussion at this meeting; and (3) the members are informed of the rule that all items must be on agenda before meeting in order for the board to be properly informed.

6. Arguments grow because the president takes sides instead of

The president appoints another board member to

	arbitrate the issue. The superintendent keeps working with the president on leadership skills.
arbitrating.	

7. Tempers flare and the discussion passes the point of productive return.

The president calls for recess or calmly summarizes points and suggests deferral until next meeting. The superintendent assists board members on handling controversy, pertinent rules of procedure, and necessary participant skills.

8. The public takes over.

The president calls for order, reminds public to address only the chair, and requests item be put on the agenda for next meeting. The superintendent recommends that board review policy on public participation to ensure that it is comprehensive and enforceable.

In order to address the issue of conducting orderly meetings, the choice could be made also to follow Examples 2 and 3 listed below by sending out such policies to the taxpayers regarding <u>charges, complaints, or challenges.</u>

<u>Example 2.</u>

<u>Charges, Complaints, or Challenges</u>

At a public meeting of the board of education, no person shall orally initiate charges or complaints against individual employees of the district or challenge instructional material used in the district. All such charges, complaints, or challenges shall be presented to the superintendent of schools in accordance with established written board policy.

We thank you for attending board meetings. We look forward to your continued interest in and support of your public schools. This support will help guarantee their excellence.

Example 3 offers still another policy on public participation.

Example 3.

All regular and special meetings of the board will be open to the public. Because the board desires to hear the viewpoints of citizens throughout the district, it will schedule one period during each meeting for public participation. It may set a time limit on the length of this period and/or a time limit for individual speakers.

Comments and questions at a regular meeting may deal with any topic related to the board's conduct of the schools. Comments at special meetings must be related to the call of the meeting.

The board president will be responsible for recognizing all speakers, maintaining proper order and adhering to any set time limits. All speakers must properly identify themselves. Questions asked by the public will, when possible, be answered immediately by the president or referred to staff members present for appropriate reply. Questions requiring investigation will be referred to the superintendent for consideration and later response.

Members of the public will not be recognized by the president as the board conducts its official business except when the board schedules in advance an interim public discussion period on a particular item.

Examples 1, 2 and 3 are offered to illustrate the need for school boards to make the choice to incorporate structure into public meetings. There must be a written policy relating to public participation at school board meetings. Without written guidelines for the public to follow, many meetings become a "free for all," especially when controversial issues are put on the agenda.

Basically, much of the unrest occurring in public education today is twofold: (1) lack of leadership on the part of management resulting in takeover by radical self-interest groups and (2) lack of financial support at the state and local levels. Lack of money and lack of leadership can cause serious destruction of our public school districts in this country. When this occurs, the district has extended an open invitation for self-interest groups to take over. If no one is at the helm addressing the challenges, who then is supposed to pilot the school district? The answer to this question is simple: Any group or groups, any individual or individuals, any legislator or legislators. When these groups continue to gain control of a school district, all operations eventually become subject to their jurisdiction. This includes personnel, building and grounds, instruction and curriculum, transportation, finance, and special services. The seeds of the groups are scattered all over the school district and the superintendent and board of education become a powerless management team. Many school districts currently are listening to the beat of the loudest drummers instead of listening to their trained professionals. When such factors exist and the control of a school district is in the hands of the wrong people, quality education declines. No longer a leader, the superintendent tries to keep everyone happy, which is a lesson in futility. The end result is superintendent burn-out or drop-out.

During the evening of the 1984 presidential election, I was watching television with interest as the Democratic Party chieftains were attempting to explain President Ronald Reagan's landslide victory over Walter

Mondale. As I listened to various people offer their accounts of what happened, I remember one gentleman saying words to the effect that "We Democrats learned a lesson. You can't cater to every special interest group and expect to come out a winner." The news commentator then said, "I am not sure I understand." The man, who had been a worker in the Democratic Party for over fifty years, said, "I simply mean we lost to the Republicans because we let the special interest groups dictate our political agenda and actions throughout the campaign. When you start promising this and that to special interest groups as we did in a national presidential campaign, you lose. You lose because when you try to listen to this group and that group, one forgets about what the real issues are in the campaign."

School administrators, especially superintendents, invite outside takeover of the school district when they spend much of their energies dodging issues and continually promising things to those that shout the loudest. Some simply don't have the courage to face up to the confrontations (challenges) that occur in the everyday operation of a school district. In my experiences as a public school administrator, I was not always the most popular person on the block. Any good leader has a goodly share of enemies. As an assistant principal, I can remember recommending expulsion for students who seriously disobeyed school policy. Parents became upset with me (putting it mildly), claiming I was ruining their daughter's or son's future. Threatening letters and phone calls came my way more than once. As I moved up the ladder of administrative responsibilities in various public school systems, the challenges increased with each advancing position. I expected performance from personnel and learned rapidly that any good organization needs competent personnel if it is to cope with the challenges in a fashion that leads to progress. I expected principals to perform and to be educational leaders. Once the course was charted annually for the school district and goals were established, I expected every administrator to model management and leadership skills in his respective position. Those who did not operate effectively were encouraged to find another career or were dismissed. Naturally, there were some

"Failure and success
go hand in hand;
you can't have one
without the other."

who thought my philosophy of management was unfair. I used to tell my principals, "If you want to consider yourself as having a good year, do something in your building that will advance education, go an extra mile, and don't worry about making mistakes as long as you learn from the experiences." I expected my management personnel to be in charge and not turn the reins over to outside groups. Trouble begins to occur when there is "all talk and no action."

Alan Loy McGinnis, in his book <u>Bringing Out the Best in People</u>, talks about the need "to be a winner." The old adage has it that "nothing succeeds like success," and Peters and Waterman in <u>In Search of Excellence,</u> their study of the best-run companies in America, found that good organizations capitalize on that truth. They believe that if employees feel that they are doing well, they will be highly motivated. So the good companies design systems that continually reinforce the notion that their people are winners, while the not so excellent companies manage to keep many of their employees constantly scrambling just to stay afloat. Parents and other stockholders of public education need to make conscientious choices about the bandwagons they are going to jump on. If self-interest groups made their schools their special interest through positive support rather than constant criticism, our schools would improve tremendously in this country.

School leaders who have schools that are successful work hard at establishing a climate where teachers and support staff know their efforts are appreciated based on the praise, support, and even financial incentives they receive. All of us like to be told that we are doing a good job by those we serve as well as by management. Inspiring are those school districts in this country which are moving forward with quality education through positive leadership practices. From some of our small rural school systems and suburban and urban districts, there are exciting happenings. From kindergarten through twelfth grade, the students are getting an education that can enable them to function in society. The reasons are varied. Primarily, it is leadership and some good management of the resources, talent, and money. The people of the farms, towns, and cities where positive things are occurring in their schools are aware of their role, the board of education's role, and the superintendent's role; and they respect and support each others responsibilities. Where good things are happening in school districts, everyone is pulling in the same direction.

Once again let me state, I am not against parents or community-minded citizens who come together as a unified group or organization to call to the attention of the board of education the need to change or take action over certain situations or issues. Some of my more rewarding endeavors as a school administrator involved meeting and working with local community groups whose main mission was to support the administration in maintaining quality education in their school system. The choice must be made to gain support by keeping the public informed of school district operations. Keeping the public well informed reduces the chance of takeover by outside groups. Asking for input is another way to build public confidence in our public schools and reduce the chance of takeover by outside groups. Such input should always be valued and implemented. Organizations familiar to all school personnel include senior citizens groups, parent-teacher organizations, retired school employees associations, Chamber of Commerce, local civic organizations, YWCA, YMCA, churches, American Cancer Society, American Heart Association, etc., and they have valued input and offer support programs. Such organizations can provide positive and constructive support including financial contributions and human resources to the school district. Through fundraising, parent-teacher associations and organizations donate millions of dollars each year in educational equipment and supplies, not to mention time and effort put into the school's fundraising activities. These kinds of organizations serve a vital part in supporting quality education in our public schools and provide a constructive way to get the total community involved.

Parents of special needs children, for example, have lobbied to have more state and federal funds earmarked to special education programs. These efforts, by and large, have brought about needed reform.

Parents have served as tutors and instructional aides in classrooms; and their efforts have been rewarding, especially for the younger children in the primary grades who need added individual attention. Many parents and community volunteers have assisted in lunch supervision, chaperoned dances, and helped with other extracurricular activities. Field trips allow parents to assist teachers as they travel to the zoos, museums, concerts and theaters. There is no doubt that organizations and parents combining together do serve our public schools in constructive and positive ways. There are very few public school officials who would turn their backs on constructive input and support from the community. The assignment of educating all children to the maximum of their ability requires a network of assistance from everyone inside as well as outside of the school district.

Albert Shanker, President of the American Federation of Teachers, said, "We're trying to do something that no other country in the history of civilization has ever tried to do. We're trying to educate every single child in this country" (To Save Our Schools, To Save Our Children, ABC).

Diane Ravitch, adjunct professor of education, Columbia Teachers College, said, "I think the biggest problem area is the number of schools that are not educating children to their fullest. They are so overburdened with responsibilities of many kinds that somehow their basic responsibility for education has been overwhelmed by all of these other needs" (To Save Our Schools, To Save Our Children, ABC).

With the task so great, as Albert Shanker points out, and the enormous burden of responsibilities upon our public schools, as Diane Ravitch noted, it seems very clear that the towns and communities across this nation can ill afford to get side-tracked by or lose control to competing self-interest groups. The choice must be made to keep control of policy making and to help keep administration in the hands of those appointed and elected to govern our public schools and to publicly support those officials, especially as we approach the demanding challenges of the 21st century.

Chapter 7

Where Do The Stockholders Fit In?

*"The nation as a whole prospers in proportion
to the level of education excellence achieved
in individual school systems. Our national
prosperity is a direct result of the dreams of
local citizens for the future of their young
people."*

--Nellie C. Weil
Past President
National School
Boards Association
America School Boards.
The Positive Power

We are the investors in today's world of public
education. Within most states, local school districts
set a tax rate which the citizens pay to support their
schools; and in paying taxes, citizens have a vested
interest in the total operations and management practices occurring in the school system. In the business
world, corporations strive to make a profit each year
so stockholders will be pleased and, in return, will
invest additional money in the company by purchasing
more stock. Besides, a good annual profit return by a
company will attract new investors who feel secure
investing in a growing and prosperous company. By
owning shares, stockholders acquire the right to have
input on various issues and policies pertaining to
overall corporate organizations and leadership. As a
part of keeping their investors informed, management
issues reports relating to the particular company's
assets vs. liabilities as well as future projections.

Stockholders (taxpayers) of public education basically have the same privileges which include the following:

- Right to voice opinions at board of education meetings;
- Right to vote on tax referenda;
- Right to vote (unless appointed) at school board elections.

The investors of public education have a big stake in deciding the future of education in this country. Their support and involvement is crucial to any local school district operation. However, in most districts, the only involvement is paying taxes. No wonder the education profession hasn't been showing good annual reports for some time. In fact, the majority of stockholders of public education receive very little information regarding financial, long-range planning forecasts. Patience is running thin and demand for change is being heard, as witnessed by the increasing number of education reform bills that are being introduced at our federal and state levels of government.

I have stated that any improvement in public education must begin at the top, starting with school board members, administrators, and deans of our educational college and university training institutions. For example, if the outcome (final product) at the university and teacher training institutions does not justify the means (expenditures), then they have only two choices: (1) convert the existing program to one of more accountability and acceptance, or (2) shift the entire training program for administrators and teachers to the public schools jurisdiction. The state of New Jersey recently took a bold step in September 1988 by adopting new standards for certification of principals. The State Board of Education of New Jersey removed the requirement that all candidates seeking certification as a principal must have had three years of teaching. Candidates may now enter the principalship without any prior teacher experience. In addition, they must pass a written test assessing their management and teaching expertise; possess a master's degree in management; and those with no prior teaching experience must teach one class a day for one year during their residency period. Also, based on the candidates level of experience, forty-five hours of formal instruction is required in the areas of curriculum and instructional supervision (<u>Education Week</u>, 14 September 1988, pp. 1-13).

Opposition to the program is predictable. The American Association of School Administrators and the New Jersey Association of School Administrators, for example, aren't happy. They claim the program downplays the importance of teaching and knowledge of education. My position is that a school administrator should have a background in both teaching and management. By position and title, a school administrator can tell others what to do, and usually they do it. That is being successful, if we determine that being successful means having tasks performed with supervision. An <u>effective</u> administrator is one who can leave the building confident that things will continue to move along. New skills are needed within the arena of the elementary/secondary principalship. A successful, effective elementary or secondary principal must have abilities in decision-making, critical thinking, establishing priorities, and communicating expectations and accountability to staff. Our education schools must employ instructors who are competent and who understand the importance of teaching, management, and leadership development. Rather than hiring business management people as school administrators, why not hire retired CEO's or part-time teachers from local corporations to lead seminars relating to developing human potential, making decisions and adopting goal-based management practices? School administration is obstacle-oriented and it requires persistent, goal-oriented, motivated, knowledgeable, enthusiastic, charismatic people to succeed in today's world of public school administration.

Demanding a quality product from our teacher-training institutions should be on the minds of every citizen in this country. When the future of our nation revolves around education, there should be nothing less than a full commitment at the national, state, and local levels supporting public education with increased funding (to produce a quality product necessitates an initial investment) and at the same time, persistently demanding accountable leadership and training. The stockholders of public education must insist that teacher-training institutions make the choice to take necessary steps to upgrade their programs in order to produce qualified professionals. There has been a severe shortage of competent teachers, especially in the science and math areas. The situation will worsen unless teaching becomes a more accountable and attractive profession.

At the local level, school districts must convince their investors that the future of public education cannot be something that is taken for granted. Teachers who can teach must be rewarded financially. Those that cannot teach must be removed. The much-debated merit pay philosophy must be addressed and dealt with, hopefully resulting in much-needed performance incentives that will keep good teachers and administrators in our schools. Administrators must exert leadership, and those that fail to do so must be removed or counseled in the area of career planning. We, the taxpayers, must see to it that school buildings and grounds are maintained and not left to decay. We build pride in young people by setting proper examples. Run-down buildings and poor upkeep of many of the elementary and secondary schools in this country send the negative message to the students, "we don't care." When the school district doesn't care, I can assure you the students won't care. The vandalism and destruction of property increases along with the cost of general maintenance. While the work places of certain tax-payers are air conditioned, carpeted, and quite attractive, too many of our children and teachers spend most of their day in crowded, noisy, dingy classrooms.

Many of our urban school districts lack the support and backing by local stockholders, primarily because many of the "supporters" have moved out to the suburbs and rural areas. State legislators must accept this fact and consider it serious enough to use their political position to increase funding legislation while at the same time demanding accountability. Currently tax reform measures to equalize funding are being finalized based on court decisions in Texas, New Jersey, Kentucky, Wyoming, Colorado, and Florida.

"School policy making
and decision making
must be based on
what's best for students."

Basically, the approach is more state aid for poor districts and less for wealthy districts with emphasis on equal education and opportunities for all children.

Suburban and rural school districts must continue to use creative public relations to ensure local stockholder support. There is a continuous fear mounting that our aging population might not support the local school system. We cannot afford to let this happen. One of the most effective ways to prevent such an occurrence is to involve our senior citizens as volunteers in our public schools. Many school districts are involving members of the business community and the benefits are felt by all.

A publication distributed by the American Association of School Administrators, Building Public Confidence in Our Schools (1983), provided the following advice:

> We can't do it alone. To be successful, our schools need the help and support of parents, non-parents, the business community and many others and the community needs us.
> When other institutions have difficulty dealing with the problems of society they inevitably "turn to the schools." Today, our educational agenda is filled with important concerns ranging from providing education for the handicapped to helping students understand the new technology.
> When schools need support, they must depend on the community for help. That's just one reason why citizens must understand the important role they must play if we are to provide excellence in education. They must see the benefits for them in higher quality schools. for example, senior citizens have a self-interest in making sure there are plenty of well-educated people making enough money to keep Social Security solvent. Business people have self-interest in assuring a well-

educated, well-trained work force with
enough earning potential to guarantee
plenty of future customers with spendable
incomes.
Coalitions can bring together many
groups in the community which share a
common interest in quality schools:
Working together with interested people
of diverse backgrounds and various walks
of life, we can better assure that our
schools are responsive to community
needs. In turn, the needs of our schools
become more apparent to citizens.
We need more than school spirit. We
need spirit for the schools. Let's make
high quality education a community
decision. Then, let's work together to
make it happen.

This pitch by the A.A.S.A. asking everyone to join
in and put confidence back in our public schools is
certainly timely. The stockholders of public education
must invest their talent, time, and energy to improve
public education in this country. With our expectations, we must also put our muscle where our mouth is:
Parent Work Days at local schools (cleaning, painting,
yard work) and tutoring programs are some of the ways
the taxpayers can put feelings into action. At the end
of each school year, if the school annual report does
not reveal growth and improvement in areas where
achievement was possible, then steps must be taken to
correct the situation. Investors of public education
should expect to receive annual reports covering the
following major operations of their school district:
student achievement scores (vs. previous year), student
attendance (vs. previous year), teacher absenteeism
(vs. previous year), financial balance (receipts vs.
income compared to previous year), dropout rate (vs.
previous year) and educational background of the professionals. These are examples of the major reports
that reveal the profit and loss statements for public
school districts.

I have repeatedly stated my concern over the lack
of decisive, positive leadership on the part of school
boards and school administrators and have mentioned my

concern relating to salaries paid to top public school officials. Similar responsibilities in the business world would bring much higher salaries. This factor must not be ignored. For example, below are budget comparisons of several Colorado school districts and similar sized Colorado corporations:

COMPARABLE SIZE
COLORADO SCHOOL DISTRICTS/COLORADO COMPANIES
1986 ANNUAL REPORT

School District/ Colorado Company	1986 Budget	Superinten- dent/CEO Salaries
Jefferson County	$317,940,126	$ 82,171
KN Energy	313,332,000	207,889
Denver	283,232,645	77,850
NBI, Inc.	282,354,000	234,000
El Paso II	104,254,143	81,000
Guaranty National	103,172,000	165,000
Boulder Valley	81,477,531	79,500
Forest Oil Company	89,275,000	229,111
Pueblo 60	65,665,375	65,000
Writer Corporation	63,930,000	178,404
Woodlin	833,555	31,000
Mesa Medical, Inc.	860,000	60,000
Ridgway	792,914	36,750
Chaparrel Resources, Inc.	778,000	60,000

Taken from Employed Persons by Detailed Industry and Major Occupations (1986).

The data indicates that the CEO in the private sector is paid approximately two to three times more compared to a school superintendent for managing a similar-sized organization.

A look at the following top salaries for large city

superintendents for the 1988-89 school year finds:

1. Richard Green, New York $150,000
2. Leonard Britton, Los Angeles. $141,800
3. Marvin Edwards, Dallas. $125,000
3. Joseph Fernandez, Miami $125,000
3. Joan Raymond, Houston $125,000

(Education Week, 7 September 1988, p. 13).

The choice must be made by the stockholders of public education to support higher salaries for top level school administrators. If the public expects schools to be run efficiently, and to produce an accountable learning product, then they must pay for such leadership.

Stockholders of our public schools must be willing to invest in their schools if things are to improve. As indicated before, investment must include our financial support as well as time and energy. However, we first must be made aware of the product we are being asked to invest in. That is why a good public relations program is needed in many school districts. We need to promote and market the many good things that are happening in our schools similar to the way successful corporations market their products.

For example, my son was recently in the market for a car. As we entered one particular dealership, we were greeted with a friendly welcome and then were escorted to the service department where we were given a tour of the facilities. Next, we were given an informative history lesson about the company by a charming salesperson. We were then involved in a human relations program whereby we were asked questions relating to preference of style, accessories, color, and interior design. Next, we were escorted to an office where we were given a lesson in car financing and were told the car would be ready for delivery the next day. The price was right, the monthly payments were within the affordable range, and my son had his first new car. We left this car dealership feeling we were treated professionally with respect and dignity and felt we knew a great deal about the quality of the product we were about to invest in. Approximately one

"The right to know,
understand, and participate
is basic to a free society
and to human dignity.
We must rekindle the
expectation that many
of our parents and
grandparents had for us--
that we prosper through
education!"

--Rudy Perpich,
Governor, Minnesota

week later, he received a letter from the president of
the corporation. The letter congratulated him on his
car purchase and thanked him for having confidence in
their product. One sentence caught my attention. "We
are most interested in your views and opinions about
your new car and the way you were treated at the local
dealership." Enclosed was a customer opinion survey
which was to be completed and returned asking for a
variety of responses relating to all phases of customer
service.

Many successful companies invest heavily in product
marketing. From beginning of sales to a year later,
the customer's input is requested and rewarded. The
end result is confidence in the company, product, and
personnel. This same approach of quality marketing
must occur in every public school throughout this
country. We need to send out school opinion surveys
annually, seeking feedback on the school's performance
from parents, former students, community leaders and
staff. We need to market a quality product known as
education to the community we serve. The initiative
for doing this must come from the local schools at the
insistence of the taxpayers. Schools and school districts must market their own quality product of education in a productive and stimulating manner, using
newspapers, radio and community cable to inform the
community of awards and achievements within the school.
New parents entering their child in school for the
first time need to be treated in the same manner that
many successful corporations treat their customers
through gestures of respect, gratitude and sincere
appreciation.

Invitations need to be sent out to parents, business leaders, senior citizens, and the community-at-
large urging them to visit schools and see educational
programs in action firsthand. At the end of the tour,
they could be offered lunch and allowed a question-and-
answer period. A special invitation should be extended
to the media. Good publicity would come out of this
simple practice. Teachers would feel rewarded because
of the interest and positive feedback received from the
community. The school district would gain favorable
publicity, heightening morale throughout the system and
gaining local support for the school district. Parents

would see needs and be better educated and motivated.
Typical of such feedback after one such tour I conducted is contained in the following letter:

> Dear Superintendent,
>
> Thank you for one of the most
> memorable days of my life. I wish every
> parent in this district would take this
> tour. I just can't stop thinking about
> the things I saw and have thought of so
> many things that I wish I had mentioned
> to you. I am looking forward to seeing
> the other part of the district after the
> holidays.
> I told Teresa T. how much we all
> enjoyed the tour and she wondered if you
> would like her to give you some
> publicity. If so, please let her know.
> I am so glad that you allowed us to
> see what kind of a place our district is.
> I am also busy trying to figure out a way
> that you will only be able to receive
> local telephone calls so no other
> district can steal you away.
> Again many, many thanks for a
> wonderful tour and most of all for giving
> us the feeling that parents might just
> know something about schools.
>
> Sincerely,
>
> Georgie D.

The local stockholders of public education must
choose to take time to become familiar with their
public schools. They must be made aware of what is
going on inside the school buildings. Investors of
public education need to be made aware where their
money is being spent.

Any successful management person will tell you, the
further a supervisor gets away from the assembly line
and the more he is separated from the workers, the more
difficult it is to know what is going on. Decision
making becomes more difficult due to a lack of famili-

arity with plan and production happenings. The workers feel they are operating in a vacuum - that no one cares. Likewise, taxpayers need to be informed of needs and made to feel welcome at the schools they are supporting.

There is even a more serious result that can occur when one loses contact with all happenings in the trenches of public education. When criticism is leveled against an instructional program, an individual's performance, or whatever, it becomes much more difficult to defend or resolve such issues if one is out of touch with the situation. A leader can't defend something unless he knows what it is he is defending. The criticism leveled against our schools today is overwhelming. Everyone has an answer to cure each of the ills. The trouble is many of the critics and skeptics attacking public education lack firsthand knowledge of the problems. They have never spent time in the hallways, cafeterias, classrooms, or neighborhood hangouts, let alone attended parent nights, sports events, concerts, plays to observe firsthand what is actually taking place. Judgements are made based on perceptions and hearsay rather than on personally gained information. Taxpayers within a school system must approach their "investment" in the same manner as a stock investor. People who invest in the financial stockmarket do so for a variety of reasons. Some desire to make short gains, while others are looking to place their money in an investment that hopefully produce increased earnings over an extended period of time. Others play the market for tax purposes; but whatever the reason or reasons, one thing is sure - before any transaction is made, the investor wants to know something about the company. He will often ask such questions as, what is the company's current status? What do future sales and earnings look like? Where does current inventory stand? What is the dividend record, past and present? What is the status of labor contracts? How much money is going into research? What is the vision of the company?

The same is true of school district stockholders. The educational world can't expect the local citizenry to support tax increases in their public school systems unless they first are made aware and understand what

they are being asked to invest in and also what the
returns will be. They must feel a sense of ownership
before they will experience a need for commitment.
Asking people to invest in their local schools is one
thing, but getting them to do it is something else.
Certain low income school districts, especially inner
city ones whose local revenues are drying up, face a
distinct disadvantage compared to their more affluent
suburban neighbors whose communities tend to support
quality education. Presently our large city schools'
only hope for increased funding is through their state
legislatures combined with local business and civic
support. A constant battle is being waged to save our
inner city school systems. A strong public relations
campaign must become top priority. There are schools
that are working in our big cities, but the average
person on the street doesn't know and doesn't care. It
is the responsibility of both parties concerned - the
schools and the taxpayers - to take the steps to bring
both sides together. Schools need to motivate parents
and businesses to want to know.

It is important that public schools choose to draw
upon business and civic leaders to assist them in
mapping a course of future growth. Business leaders
and organizations must decide to get behind their local
school districts and work as a team to address the
challenges that lie ahead. Companies must choose to
improve public education by lobbying legislatures for
reform, providing disadvantaged students with jobs as
incentives to graduate, and support tax increases.
Community organizations and city governments must roll
up their sleeves and dig in to fight the battle of
pessimism and despair over public education in America,
especially the blight that is currently hovering over
urban education. In Palo Alto, California, the city
government, in conjunction with the school district,
has arranged a joint partnership to bring financial
relief to the school district. The plan calls for
leasing unused school facilities to the city for
before-and-after school day-care programs, community
arts programs and additional office space. The school
district will receive $3 million in utility tax rev-
enues and $900,000 in lease income annually (Education
Week, 3 May 1989, p. 13). Similar organizations and
companies benefit in such an arrangement. Large com-

panies want to move where education is working and where they don't have to spend their money teaching employees things they should have learned in school. It would also allow their employees to feel good about the school situation for their children. Battles must be fought for higher salaries, improved staff performance, and revised formulas for funding our local school districts. Boards of education must open their doors to local civic and business organizations and let them have a taste of the happenings in the classrooms. Many will come to realize there are tremendous advancements being made in public classrooms throughout this country, some against overwhelming odds. International Business Machine recently invested $25 million in the form of grants to selected schools of education and school districts. The recipients will receive laboratories of personal computers, software, and technical support, plus training and travel expenses. Other companies, such as Apple Computer Inc. and Franklin Computer Corporation, also have been involved in similar grant programs to schools (Education Week, 10 May 1989, p. 1). More companies need to make the choice to support and promote public education at the local, state, and national levels in this country. When the business community takes an active role in supporting schools and communities are actively involved in their schools, education flourishes.

Several years ago in an ABC documentary, To Save Our Schools, To Save Our Children, correspondent Marshall Frady, said:

> To recover the faith of business leaders, of the community of middle-class parents, public schools like Southwest (Southwest High School, Kansas City, Missouri) must prove they can prepare students for any university in this country. In Southwest's battle for community support, every personal success becomes a school triumph.

Continuing, Frady said,

> At risk here is whether the clash between politicians demanding stricter

measurements of teacher quality and
teacher unions resisting them will so
reduce and embitter the issues that the
nation will lose sight of the need for
more difficult but fundamental reforms.
The politicians may be in danger of
advertising quick fixes. Some unions may
have entered into a disastrous political
myopia by resisting popular reform like
competency testing and merit pay, eroding
public willingness to address the large
imperatives for reform. So a collision
is building. State legislatures have
made it clear: Any action on teacher
problems will only be bought by guarantee
of teacher quality.

Marshall Frady's comments are worth digesting. As
I have stated, the educator can't expect the stockholders of public education in this country to shell
out more money for public education unless they see
certain advancements and a promise for the future.
Some school districts currently are having qualified
financial planners and developers from the business
community to oversee school district operations. This
is good management and makes sense, especially if the
present leadership lacks those skills. That is why it
is so important to elect or appoint members to the
school board who have a vision, are goal oriented, and
are aware of the ingredients that are needed to cause
organizational advancement. It is much easier to
attract investors to public education when they observe
a solid management team at the top which is making
things happen in the best interest of the students,
parents, and community.

Obviously there have been school board elections
where candidates desiring a seat on the board promised
easy answers to problems. Heading the list of promises
in many school district elections today involves firing
the superintendent and improving student test scores.
Besides having candidates seeking a seat on the board
of education who do not have the best interest of the
school system at heart or "crusaders" campaigning to
overhaul (overthrow) the school system, the next worst
thing occurring in school board elections is to have a

split board as a result of an election. This means one side will vote one way while the other side will vote just the opposite, with the superintendent of schools caught in the crossfire. Such situations can ruin a school district in rapid fashion. A simple agenda item will result in split voting simply because it is a way of exerting power on behalf of one group of school board members over the other.

Stockholders in today's world of public education must choose to do all in their power to prevent this from occurring in their local school districts. In many of our cities and towns, the Monday night school board meeting not only offers the best show in town, it's free. In Chapter 4, tips were offered suggesting effective ways of conducting school board meetings. As stated before, under a split school board situation, self-interest groups will rise to the top and dominate the meetings. School boards must prevent such occurrences by annually doing a self-assessment of their leadership performances. A grant from the Kellogg Foundation is allowing Michigan to finance just such an assessment. In addition, seeking input from local taxpayers should also become a part of each school board's annual evaluation process. Unfortunately, seeking input from the community comes only at times, in some school districts, when there is a need to generate support for a tax increase for higher teacher salaries or the building of new schools. Such a one-sided process of asking for support is bad management. A major reason why so many requests for school tax hikes are turned down is simply because no one has kept the investors informed of happenings in the school district except when the request goes out for more money. If a tax increase is not approved, usually school district officials will state the negative outcomes, including overcrowding of pupils, additional layoff of personnel, program cutbacks, curtailment of extra-curricular events, and so on and so forth. In order to seek passage of the tax hike, the investors are threatened with negative results if they don't go along with approving higher taxes. This is an attempt to shift the blame and responsibility from the school district to the stockholders.

A school system that communicates positive, excit-

"People who fail to
establish and work
towards goals end
up going nowhere."

ing happenings on a regular basis (resulting in a well-
informed public), coupled with a unified board of
education, has a better chance of gaining additional
tax revenue from the local stockholders to finance
public school operations than one that does not. The
investors in public education want a quality product.
They expect children who enter their public schools to
be educated. They expect their schools to do their
job; and if they've been kept informed, they'll be
willing to pay for it.

The local stockholders of public education in this
country have come out strong on several key issues
recently. According to the June 1989 Phi Delta Kappan,
recent polls have found that the stockholders of public
education favor merit pay by a 4-to-1 margin. Teachers
oppose it by a 2-to-1 margin, citing such reasons as
difficulty by administrators in evaluating teachers and
possible morale problems. I believe that merit pay can
work, but the way it has been handled in some school
districts has been a disaster. Merit pay must be based
on teaching performance and not on superficial responsibilities like assuming extracurricular activities or
taking a course at a university. How well the individual teacher performs in the classroom must be the
main criteria for judging below average, average, and
above average performances. The question is, who will
do the evaluating, and how is it to be administered?
We administrators have fumbled the ball on this one and
we know it. School boards need to tackle this issue
and not dodge it. I am of the opinion that the general
public is not about to give in on this issue of merit
pay. The stockholders of public education associate
merit pay with bringing about improved performance.
Individual goal-designed formats of evaluation that
address professional competency and growth, as well as
illustrate incompetency, must become a reality. Such
designs serve as a foundation for building acceptable
merit pay programs. Teachers should be evaluated based
on a format similar to the MBO design I suggested for
administrators (Chapter 4). Teachers, like administrators, should have individual evaluation plans based on
district/school program needs plus incorporating performance objectives that address the strengths as well
as the weaknesses of each individual teacher. Once
this is done, then total performance can be assessed of

all teachers and compared to individual as well as
building goals.

School boards have failed to exert the demand for
teacher quality. Too many boards of education and
their attorneys have claimed that continuous documen-
tation is needed before steps can be taken to remove a
teacher; consequently, the most that is usually done is
some type of remediation that will hopefully result in
improved teacher performance. The fact is, some
teachers simply can't teach, regardless of how much
help they receive. The result of having them continue
to teach in our public schools is permanent emotional
and intellectual damage to many students. Unfortunately, principals lack the substantive knowlege of
directing incompetent as well as marginal teachers
towards improved performance. The routine practice is
to observe, check yes or no as to whether the teaching
skill was performed or not, and then add up the boxes.
If more of the boxes contain yes, then the teacher is
judged competent. What teachers learn to do is put on
the "show" when it's time for their evaluation visit.
After the visitation, many teachers in our school rooms
fall back to mediocre teaching. Therefore, below
average teachers continue to teach in our public
schools at the expense of the public stockholders.
Even more serious is what teacher malpractice is doing
to the students. Students of today's public school
systems entering classrooms of teachers who are below
par have limited their chances for a future in the 21st
century. Employees that land jobs in major corporations have to be retrained. Corporate executives are
asking educators, "Why should this country pay twice to
educate her children?"

The people who pay the taxes to support our public
schools must understand that issues relating to the
improvement of our public schools are vast and complex,
but not so insurmountable that we can't pave the way
for improvement.

Besides these concerns and needs for improvement,
there is also another dangerous situation occurring in
classrooms throughout this country that stockholders
need to act upon. During the time that I served as
superintendent in Aurora, Illinois, Ben Wilson, a 17-

year-old Simeon Vocational High School senior in
Chicago died of gunshot wounds in a sidewalk shooting
near his school during a lunch break. Two 16-year-old
youths from a neighboring high school admitted to the
shooting. Wilson met his death through the use of an
unregistered .22-caliber pistol. What brought this
incident national attention was that this youth was a
6'8" superstar basketball player. The two 16-year-olds
stated the motive was robbery. According to reports,
the shooting took place as Wilson was walking with his
girlfriend and another girl to a store near their
school during lunchbreak when he bumped into the two
youths. An argument ensued which quickly turned into
attempted robbery. An eyewitness close to the scene
reported Wilson saying, "Excuse me." And one of the
youths said to him, "There ain't going to be no excuses," and shot him. Named to the United Press International 1984 all-state tournament first team, Wilson
was highly recruited by major university basketball
powers. His inspiring life came to an abrupt end at
the hands of two teens who reportedly were members of a
local street gang.

Day in and day out, teachers in classrooms in our
public schools are facing serious and dangerous situations never before encountered in public education.
Violent acts of crimes are occurring among adolescent
teenagers, much of which is gang related. The activities of gangs, especially those in our larger cities,
spill over into the classrooms of our elementary,
junior and senior high schools. As one teacher who
teaches in a junior high school in a suburb of Chicago
recently said to me, "Ten years ago, I enjoyed
teaching. It was such a rewarding profession for me to
witness students turned on to learning. Now, I consider my day successful if I can just make it safely to
school and back without bodily harm and personal
injury."

Many of our classroom teachers and administrators
are at the mercy of defenseless and uncontrollable acts
of classroom violence with nowhere to turn. Teacher
assault cases are increasing, and student absenteeism
is a constant problem. Rebellion against authority is
a common practice in many of our public schools. These
kinds of acts must not be tolerated. Schools must work

with parents and local and state law enforcement
agencies to curb such violence within the halls and
classrooms of our public schools. They can do this by
employing trained law enforcement personnel to work in
the schools. There is nothing wrong educationally,
socially, or psychologically for the school district to
choose to employ police counselors where acts of
student and gang violence are occurring. In fact, my
own experience with having police counselors in schools
was extremely beneficial. The arrangements were
simple. The city paid half of the counselor's salary,
and the school district paid the other half. Each
counselor had an office in his respective school and
was involved with student counseling, initiating
preventive in-school measures to reduce violent juvenile acts, and working with administrators, teachers,
and parents in conjunction with the local police
department in offering out of school programs aimed at
increasing the self esteem of high risk students who
were potential dropouts. Students evaluated their
association and relationship with each counselor as
very high because they had a friend, confidante, and
advocate they could trust and confide in. During the
summer months, each police counselor assumed his
regular duties within the city police department.
Another fringe benefit of the program was the police
counselors were always present at all extra-curricular
activities put on by the school. I think it would be a
wise choice for troubled schools to investigate such a
program. The cost is not that prohibitive, and the
benefits to students, teachers, administrators and the
community at large is tremendous.

Stockholders of public education should keep in
mind that violent acts of juvenile crimes occur in
rural and suburban schools as well. The smaller school
districts are not immune to such incidents. When one
realizes, for example, that 12 percent of America's
teenagers admit to being into "polydrugs" (combining
alcohol with other drugs), it is little wonder that our
school buildings continue to serve as battlegrounds for
teenage violence (Chicago Tribune, 8 September 1984,
Sec. 1, p. 2).

Many of the students engaged in discipline problems
in our schools come from broken homes. A broken home

doesn't necessarily mean that the parents are divorced, separated, or deceased. A broken home can also mean both parents are happily married but, unfortunately, have lost touch with their children. We have a nation of latch-key children regardless of whether they are in a single-parent home or not. The trend today finds more and more parents delegating the responsibility of raising their children to "others," including and especially the school. There was a time if a student was disciplined at school, he would be disciplined again at home. Few parents provide such follow through and support these days. Many put their own personal lives and everyday interests ahead of the responsibility of raising their children. With increasing numbers of both parents working, teachers and school administrators have little if any room to turn to for home-front support.

According to estimates in the Seneca Journal Tribune (20 August 1988), 60 percent of today's 4-year olds will live in a single parent home before they turn 18. Drug abuse by U. S. teenagers is the highest among developed nations. Today, 40 percent of public school students are minorities, and nearly one quarter of all children live below the poverty level (a family of four living on an annual income of less than $11,203).

Some parents find it easier to blame someone else or agency for their child's misbehavior rather than assume full responsibility and try to do something about it. Such parents attack school discipline policies and school administrators rather than support them. "Latch-key" children are children who are regularly left without direct parental supervision before or after school. It comes as no surprise when experts tell us there are millions of latch-key children in America today. Reports in the December 1984 Phi Delta Kappan estimate that approximately half of the 13 million children aged 13 and under will lack direct supervision during some portion of the day. Children who are home alone in the morning many times will miss the bus, since no one is there to wake them and prepare them for school. Such children at times will call their parent at work and complain they don't feel well, creating an excuse for not going to school. Although schools cannot solve all of society's problems, I do

"Public education will
not improve through
a quick fix,
but an accountable fix."

feel that it would be a wise choice for school districts to provide before and after school care for
latch-key children. It is my feeling that a majority
of parents would rather pay the schools for additional
skill development, etc. and be responsible for transportation to and from school, than to have their
children come home (or not come directly home) to an
empty house to watch television and be left unsuper-
vised for three to four hours every school day. Teachers could earn extra pay on their main job site rather
than driving elsewhere to take an extra job as many of
them currently are doing. What would happen during
these before and after hours would be up to the
particular needs of the community. For example, these
hours could include tutoring, library work, as well as
adjunct classes in aerobics, piano, voice, band,
crafts, elocution, sewing, cooking, ballroom dancing,
social graces, religions of the world, drawing, peer
counseling, drama, and supervised homework. Addressing
the latch-key children issue presents a host of
challenges for public school educators and an issue
that must be dealt with since all indicators point to
an increasing number of such children entering our
schools well into the 21st century.

These are just a few of the challenges that face
public school teachers and administrators on a daily
basis. Stockholders of public education need to be
made aware of what is going on out on the frontlines of
public education in this country. Once made aware,
they can be asked to support school programs in a
variety of ways, including the support of programs
designed to help children learn before or after regular
school hours. In some parts of the country, the classroom activities continue on the school bus because in
some states, like Texas and Montana, students spend two
hours or more each day riding a bus to and from school.
Special instruction could be implemented to students
who need remedial help. There is no legal reason why
the schools have to shut down at 3 to 4 p.m. daily.
Many teachers would rather stay two extra hours at
school for extra pay than to hop in the car and drive
fifty miles away to their second job. The American
taxpayers need to take personal responsibility for what
is happening in education and support teachers emotionally as well as financially. An outstanding example of

taxpayers support is taking place in Atlanta, Dallas, and many other cities, where a group of businessmen are willing to put their dollars where their mouths are by promising sixth graders that if they do well in school, they will pay their way through college.

So the stockholders of public education must look at the total picture of American public education today and the complexities that picture represents. As noted before, it takes a good quality product to sell to the investor - a product that offers a future; a product that attracts investors. The product of public education as we know it today unfortunately has not been attracting many investors. The list of concerns that need to be addressed seems never ending, and as someone mentioned to me recently, "trying to correct the problems in American public education is like trying to repair an old bed spring - you get one spring fixed and another pops up."

Credit must be given for bringing the current issues of public education before the public through the various national reform packages starting with the Nation at Risk. This report, and others which have followed, calls for tougher standards for students and teachers; more science, math, and computer instruction; a longer school day; more homework; and dropout prevention. Certainly such reports are long overdue.

> ...The average graduate of our
> schools and colleges today is not as
> well-educated as the average graduate of
> 25 or 35 years ago, when a much smaller
> proportion of our population completed
> high school and college. The negative
> impact of this fact...cannot be
> overstated.

We have lots of reports telling us what the problems are, but few schools making the changes needed to help solve those problems.

The stockholders of public education need to make a choice and that is to visit their local buildings and classrooms and observe firsthand the strengths as well as the weaknesses. This is where the foundation lies, and it is here that the first step must be taken. To begin the rebuilding job of public education, educators must provide a continuing information program that reaches beyond the professional staff. It must be directed toward the total community - the businesses, the retired, the city planners, the families - asking for their support, input and service. Listening and responding to needs, as well as keeping people informed, is basic to the existence of any democratic institution.

The initiation of such action, including planning and encouraging people from the community to join in the cause to address the priorities of public education at local, state, and national levels, should be under the guidance and direction of school board members and school administrators working as a team.

It seems that when there is a problem in public education, the first thing educators do is form a committee. This is good public relations in many instances, but goes only half-way in resolving issues. School districts must choose to incorporate action-based committees, primarily made up of teachers/administrators as well as representatives from the general business and community areas, and assign them the charge of presenting recommendations to their local, state and national school officials and help to follow through on making goals become a reality.

Several major issues confronting public education in this country requiring immediate attention are:

1. Large city school districts are too large to expect effective results. There is a need to divide large urban school systems into individual smaller and separate school systems.

2. States must adequately provide a fair and equitable formula for funding local school districts. Allocation of state and federal funds should be based on potential local effort (local tax base and income of families) and what it costs to educate a child in each school district.

3. <u>State Departments of Education are becoming increasingly bureaucratic.</u> There is a need to decentralize each State Department of Education into regional centers throughout each state in order to (1) serve the needs of the local districts better and (2) reduce bureaucracy.

4. <u>Violence in the classroom is increasing.</u> Disciplinary procedures within the school must be tightened up and more responsibility placed on parents for controlling the behavior of their child. Schools must write definite policies and inform students and parents of the expectations and consequences.

5. <u>Public education, in general, lacks an informed citizenry.</u> Schools and school districts need to launch an effective public relations program that causes stockholders to become excited and supportive of their schools with the same zest and zeal that is generated by Americans towards their local high school and college football teams. We must promote and market public education using the same marketing techniques and ideas practiced by successful corporations.

In addition, each local school district has its own unique issues that need to be resolved - declining revenue and enrollments, desegregation, conservation of energy, building upkeep, transportation, grading, and course offerings - just to name a few. Add these individual district issues to the global concerns facing all school districts, as well as higher education in this country; and one can see the magnitude of challenges facing public education today.

Professor Diane Ravitch of Columbia Teachers College put the responsibility of public education squarely on the shoulders of the stockholders by stating the following in ABC's documentary <u>To Save Our Schools, To Save Our Children</u>.

This is an incredible society. It's a wonderful governmental system that we

> have, and we have a long record, a
> century and a half of leading the world
> in popular education. I can't believe
> we're going to let ourselves down by not
> having the kinds of schools that we want.
> It's not easy, but I think it's a
> challenge that's worthy of a country that
> has led the world in universal education
> throughout the 19th and 20th centuries.

Charles Silberman in <u>Crisis in the Classroom</u> (1970)
stated the following some two decades ago:

> The remaking of American education
> will not be possible without a new kind
> of public dialogue in which all
> interested parties join. It will not be
> possible, moreover, unless we go beyond
> dialogue. Students, parents, teachers,
> administrators, school board members,
> college professors, taxpayers - all will
> have to act, which means that all will
> have to make difficult decisions; that
> the road to reform is always uphill.

The public can't expect results sitting in the
stands. The public can't expect results by yelling and
screaming what should be done to improve our education
system and yet never have stepped foot inside a school
room door. The public can't expect results by just
pumping more money into the hands of those that cry the
hardest without demanding accountability. The public
can't expect improvements in local school districts
that are controlled by selfish interest groups. The
public can't expect results at any level of public
education unless there is leadership at the top.
School administrators can't expect support for public
education unless the public feels confident in the
product. And, finally the public can't expect improved
staff morale and increased performance unless effective
marketing and evaluation formats are functioning.

The eternal flame of good happenings in our public
schools is still burning, but the fuel supply is
getting low. The American public must make the choice
to not let this flame go out. Alvin Toffler, in <u>Future</u>

Shock (1970), stated:

> It would be a mistake to assume that
> the present-day educational system is
> unchanging. On the contrary, it is
> undergoing rapid change. But much of
> this change is no more than an attempt to
> refine the existent machinery, making it
> ever more efficient in pursuit of
> obsolete goals. The rest is a kind of
> browning motion, self-canceling,
> incoherent, directionless. What has been
> lacking is a consistent direction and a
> logical starting point.

The 1970 words of Toffler on education necessitate a new and consistent direction of accountability as we head into the 21st century in public education. The solid fibers of our education system must be preserved. The good teachers that teach our children and the good administrators that lead as well as manage our schools and school districts provide the basis for preserving the solid roots of what public education is all about. However, they need the backing and support of the stockholders in order to continue. The choice to invest human and financial resources into a lifetime venture such as public education is well spent, providing the returns are paying dividends. There are still too many Americans that fail to see the importance of supporting public education. Too many of us will spend twenty or thirty dollars at a restaurant, yet turn down a fifteen dollar increase annually to support a school referendum. Incidentally, school budget support would be easier for the public to understand if the request for money was made in manageable terms. For example, instead of asking the public for $5 million, say, "For an increase of just $15.00 a year per household, we can finish the new school, gym, library, or hire x number of teachers to reduce classroom size."

As we move into the 21st century, one must ask, will our investment returns in public education get better or worse? We do know that without a good return for each dollar spent on public education, the taxpayers will reflect their frustrations by their vote on school bond issues and their personal involvement. There are too many other competing forces within our society who want the public education dollar. Unless the product of public education continues to improve, then education in the 21st century will not attract the needed stockholders to support our schools in this country. We cannot afford to let this happen.

Chapter 8

Your Choice: Private or Public Education?

"We all have the same goal and we all must recognize that this nation cannot progress until everyone is educated."

--Lauro F. Cavazos
Secretary of Education
taken from <u>Education Week</u>, 2 November 1988

Several years ago, I came across the following direct mail sent out to parents from Providence-St. Mel High School, a private school located on the west side of Chicago, titled "Investing in a Miracle." I have extracted excerpts from the letter to show how one inner city private school faces up to the challenges of urban education.

Dear Friend:

What does it take to change a bitter, poor, tough, street-wise kid into a respected, contributing member of society? <u>The answer may just very well be found in the remarkable story I'm about to tell you.</u>

Providence-St. Mel is a private high school on Chicago's West Side, unlike any other school you've ever heard about.

Providence-St. Mel is located in the heart of the part of Chicago people drive through with their car doors locked and their windows up tight. Generally, the people inside the car are "up tight" too, until they get out of the neighborhood. They know that these streets are ruled by gangs, prostitutes and drug dealers. And through those tightly rolled-up windows, they can see some of the most devastating poverty to be found anywhere in the United States.

The students at Providence-St. Mel, far from being pampered or rich, are desperately poor black kids--kids who have been dealt their cards from the bottom of the deck.

They're plain, ordinary kids--no more endowed with beauty, brains or athletic ability than any other group. In fact, if you met them before they came to Providence-St. Mel, you'd probably be rather unimpressed with their potential. That's where the miracle comes in!

Before I explain how the miracle occurred, let me tell you what the miracle is.

In 1982 and in 1983, every single graduate of Providence-St. Mel went on to college! And earlier graduates have established a resounding record of success both in college and their chosen careers.

And the graduates of Providence-St. Mel don't go on to "easy" schools. They're at places like Princeton, Northwestern, University of Chicago, Howard University, Creighton University, University of Wisconsin, Illinois Institute of Technology, and the like.

By now, you're probably curious what
the secret is. The answer may be partly
found in the school's nickname:
Providence-St. Mel -- "the Hard Work High
School."

Motivation, Discipline and Hard Work
make the difference. These are the three
secrets of Providence-St. Mel. They're
the tools which help turn street kids
into doctors, engineers, and middle-class
taxpayers--even if they come from
families who have been on welfare for
three or four generations.

. Motivation begins with belief in
one's self. The pupils at PSM gain more
than academic knowledge. They discover
that, through their own efforts, they can
change their lives. To strengthen this
motivation, Providence-St. Mel offers an
unusual reward for achievement. When a
student achieves the honor roll, the
school refunds part of the tuition for
that quarter. The check is not made out
to a parent--the parent didn't get the
A's--it's made out to the student who
earned them.

. Discipline teaches the students to
"play by the rules." The rules are
strict and the penalties severe. Cut a
class and you must pay a $20 fine (and
bring in your parents to get you
reinstated). Cut another class and
you're gone for good. Smoke dope on
school property and you're ex-
pelled--along with anyone who's with you.
"Forget" your homework repeatedly and mop
a floor after school. These rules and
others like them are not constraints on
serious students. They simply create the
environment that is necessary for
success. So there is no dope. There are
no gangs. And the only painting on the
walls is done by art students.

. Hard Work: That's where Motivation and Discipline pay off. The ladder out of poverty is education. The better the education, the sturdier the ladder. And to get that education, the most important component is hard work. The students at Providence-St. Mel have to work even harder than the students at other schools. When they first arrive at PSM, most of them are academically well below grade level. They lack the important reading and mathematical skills which form the basis for successful college preparation. It takes a lot of hard work, a lot of studying and homework, to make up for those past deficiencies and become academically competitive with the graduates of those rich suburban schools. Obviously, the students do their homework. Otherwise, 100% of the last two graduating classes would not have been accepted--and many given scholarships--at colleges and universities all across America. Most of all, the students learn one of life's most important lessons--one which will remain with them long after graduation. Each and every graduate knows from personal experience that "Hard work really pays off."

... Providence-St. Mel High
School, 119 South Central
Park, Chicago, IL 60624

Providence-St. Mel's call to "Invest in a Miracle" is legitimate and shows what can be done when there is a commitment in keeping education the number one school priority. This particular private school, with which I am somewhat familiar after having lived in the Chicago area, tolerates no foolishness, maintains a fair, strict, consistent discipline code and has a dedicated faculty.

Providence-St. Mel proves that inner city schools

"Establishing and communicating expectations keeps school districts alive and progressing."

can be successful and the major reasons for its success
are easily identified:

- Dedicated administration and faculty
- No-nonsense administered discipline
- Basic curriculum
- No radical special interest group
  intervention
- Active alumni program
- Highly respected sports program
- Active guidance program
- Individualized instruction

Providence-St. Mel, as well as other private
schools, is not faced with the mandates and bureaucracy
that confronts our public schools. Many of this
country's private schools are producing educated
students that have a future in front of them. The
unique feature of Providence-St. Mel is that they are
doing a superb job of educating a student body that is
similar to those found in many of our public schools.
This particular private school has many similarities to
urban public schools. Most private schools have a
majority of white upper middle class students coming
from homes whose parents have advanced degrees. Not so
for Providence-St. Mel. This particular private school
has a student body originating out of the streets and
alleys of urban housing.

According to the U.S. Department of Education News
(1989), in 1980 there were approximately 301,000
elementary and secondary private school teachers in
this country. In the fall of 1989, 352,000 were
teaching in private elementary and secondary schools.
Up until the recent reform movements over public
education were issued, an increasing number of children
were attending parochial, nonsectarian, or other
schools outside the public system according to a 1984
U. S. Department of Education report. Claiming an
undercounting of private school enrollment in the
1980's, the National Center for Education Statistics in
1984 reported that "one in every eight American
children .... attends a private school" (Chicago
Tribune, 20 December 1984). In the fall of 1987, there
were 5.3 million (11.7 percent of the 45.3 million
students in all U. S. elementary and secondary schools)

attending 26,000 private schools. The 5.3 million private school enrollment figure for 1987 becomes interesting when compared to 1980. In 1980 as in 1987, 5.3 million students in this country (11.5 percent of the 46.3 million students in all schools) were attending 24,500 private schools.

The issue over superiority of private schools vs. public schools is an interesting one. Reviewing the 1986 National Assessment of Education Progress in <u>Education Week</u> (2 November 1988), the private schools edge in student achievement over public schools "is not that wide," according to Chester E. Finn, the former Assistant Secretary of Education. For example, the N.A.E.P. reading, history and literature assessments reported in the November 1988, issue of <u>Education Week</u> revealed that "3rd graders scored 5 points higher than their public school counterparts on the math part of the test and 4 points higher in science on a 500 point scale. Private school 7th graders scored 14 points higher in math and 17 points higher in science." According to Mr. Finn, the narrowing of the gap of student achievement scores by public school students vs. their private school counterparts during the past several years originates in public school students taking the "core" academic courses.

The public must remember that when private schools state their superiority over public schools there are several things to keep in mind. First, when comparing anything to something else, be consistent in the comparisons. It is not possible to compare differences and claim one is better than the other. To say that one program is better than the other can only be done when like variables are compared to other like variables. This same application applies to private vs. public education comparisons. Second, public schools in this country must take every student who comes knocking at the door with the only stipulations being they have established guardianship and live within the boundaries of the school system. Private schools, basically, have the right to reject any student who seeks enrollment. Therefore, results of private vs. public education comparisons on who is "doing the better job" can be misleading. Take, for example, the following illustration.

	Private A School	Public A School
Location	Inner-City	Inner-City
Enrollment	2,000	2,100
Grade	9-12	9-12
Mean I.Q.	112	92
Parents Level of education	95% graduated (high school)	52% graduated (high school)
	55% four-year degrees	10% four-year degrees
Percent going on to 4-year college program	92%	28%
Income of Parents	Upper middle	Low middle, Low
Faculty Advanced degrees	58%	57%
Total Achievement Test Results (California Test of Basic Skills)	93% (mean score)	58% (mean score)

In looking at the above illustration at a glance, one might conclude Private (A) School is doing a better job of educating its students. We have 92% of the total student body from Private (A) School going on to some type of four-year college program compared to only 28% for Public (A) School. It looks as though the students from Private (A) School are better prepared academically for life on the higher education campuses, and they could possibly be.

The mean achievement test scores are something else to look at in comparing private to public education. Here again we have Private (A) School with a score of 93% while Public (A) School has a low of 58%. Students in Private (A) School are doing much better on their standardized achievement tests than their counterparts in Public (A) School. Does this mean that teachers in Private (A) School are better teachers? All kinds of questions can be raised. For example, are the students in Private (A) School "smarter" than the students in Public (A) School? Neither example indicates teacher turnover rates, the amount of time spent on basic instruction, nor parent support, all of which are key variables in determining school performance. Again, one must be extremely careful in comparing the benefits of private education and public education in this country. Keep in mind that the main ingredient of what makes any public or private school work or not work is the combined performance of the paid professionals.

Certainly a 10-point spread in mean IQ scores shows something about the ability of students at each of the two schools. The overall student body at Private (A) School has a broader base of knowledge than the students from Public (A) School suggesting that test scores should be higher in Private (A) School vs. Public (A) School and they are. Does this mean better teaching is going on in the private school? Not necessarily! One possibility our illustration suggests is that public school students have not been exposed to an enriching, supporting, educational environment at home as much as private students have been since the educational level of private school parents having post-secondary degrees is higher. There could be outstanding teaching going on in the public school, possibly even better than in the private school; however, the results do not necessarily show up in the box score primarily because the educational level of the students is lower.

When various private school educators claim superiority of their programs over the public schools, I remind them that it might be a good idea to turn the tables and have the students from the various public schools enroll for one semester at various private schools and vice-versa. If teachers can teach, they can teach anyone, anyplace, anytime - provided the subject or grade level relates to their area of expertise. Suburban private schools, for example, have mainly the "cream of the crop" students with parents who are willing to pay for and support their child's education. If we scan educational research findings over the last decade, we find several interesting conclusions regarding parental influence on a child's academic progress in school.

- Achievement in school is directly related to socio-economic level of parents.
- Parents of children who have

> attended post-secondary education
> programs (i.e., college obtained
> advanced degrees, etc.) by and
> large lend support and become
> more involved in their child's
> education.

These two factors play a major role in determining academic progress of students.

As stated before, when valid comparisons are undertaken, one must compare "likes to likes." For example, take Private School (A) and compare it to another almost identical Private School (A); then a true comparison can be made. If I wanted to assess student test scores in Private School (A) to determine if the school is achieving as it should, then I would want to find another private school that is similar. Enrollments, socio-economic level of parents, age, sex, IQ scores, etc., would have to match up in similarity before any study could begin.

Private and public school educators should do more comparing to schools of like nature and less comparing to unlike schools, be they private or public. When one takes affluent private suburban schools and compares student achievement results to an inner-city public school, naturally the private school scores will be higher. But I would never claim that better teaching is taking place in the private school. Based on the type of students and backgrounds that teachers have to cope with in our inner city public schools, many are doing a superb job. Challenges most often bring out the best in people.

Take for example Woodrow Wilson High School in Washington, D. C., with a student population of 1,500 (60 percent are black; 20 percent international, mostly Asian and Hispanic; and 20 percent are white) with a student-teacher ratio of 25 to 1. This public school, like others, demonstrates that a public school can work even against tremendous odds. For example, in 1988, Wilson High placed its seniors at every Ivy League university, plus some other 100 colleges throughout the country. Many of the more elite parents of the D. C. area bypass Woodrow Wilson High and end up sending their children to the more elite private schools in the area. They do so because, like so many other parents, they feel the public schools, especially those located in large downtown cities, are gang and drug infested, unsafe, and failing to prepare kids for college. Since public schools are plagued with the ills of the society, they are to be commended for withstanding discipline problems while, at the same time, striving to educate those who attend. My own children, for example, have received both inner city education and suburban education, all in the public school sector. I can honestly say that it would be very difficult for me to distinguish which environment provided the best educational package now that all three have graduated from college. However, I can draw several comparisons from both settings.

1. Both public school settings (urban and suburban) had strong, decisive administrator leadership.
2. In both settings, there was a minority of incompetent teachers protected by tenure and seniority.
3. The majority of the teachers in both settings knew their subject and could teach effectively.
4. The inner city setting revealed that minority students, as well as white students, have parents who expect and require discipline at home as well as at school.

The inner city system somehow brought out a greater awareness and understanding for the less fortunate. Our son, for example, played basketball both in high school and in college. He appreciated his association with the majority of less fortunate (based on financial and parental support) players on the team. They ate, slept, socialized and played well together on the basketball court. I can honestly say I am proud my children had the opportunity to associate with friends, black and white, who were honest, well-behaved, mature, hardworking and whose parents/parent instilled in them the difference between right and wrong. It was always a pleasure to have young adults of this caliber in our home.

"Setting expectations
is the heart valve that
keeps school districts
alive and progressing."

Enrollment of public school children in private schools was increasing up until several years ago. Recent reports, however, reveal a reduction in total private school enrollments throughout the country, primarily because of the national reform movements occurring in public education. Parents who elect to send their children to private schools usually do so because they have become dissatisfied with their local public schools over such things as ineffective leadership, reduction of funds, sub-par teaching, teacher strikes, cutback in programs, busing, rising taxes, and poor discipline.

Private schools are basically of two types, religious and independent. The majority of religious schools are affiliated with the Roman Catholic Church. The next largest number are supported by the Lutheran Church, and the third are Jewish schools.

Deciding between elementary-secondary private education and public education must be treated with full knowledge, understanding, and objectivity. A comparison of student achievement scores between non-public schools and public schools is possible providing socio-economic levels are similar, including the comparison of the number of students on the full and reduced lunch program. If I were in the market of choosing a private school for my child, I would consider the following areas before I made my decision:

(1) Leadership qualities (Is the school working?)
(2) Test scores (by subject area)
(3) Class size
(4) Staff evaluation procedures and the handling of staff incompetency
(5) Student's perception of teaching staff
(6) Current instructional and program priorities
(7) Expenditure per pupil
(8) Philosophy of school
(9) Discipline policies
(10) Educational background of staff
(11) Tuition cost
(12) Extra-curricular program

By following the above checklist, a parent can determine if private education is the best product for his child. Some parents forego making any conscientious assessment and force private education on their children when some would be better off academically, emotionally, physically, and socially in a public school setting. Just because dad or mom or brother or sister chose to attend a private school doesn't mean a younger brother or sister should automatically follow in their footsteps.

In most religious and independent schools, there is no question that, in general, student discipline is better than in public schools. But once again in religious and independent schools, they are teaching students who come from homes with parents supportive enough to pay twice (taxes and tuition) for their children's education. They support discipline and that, too, makes a big difference.

Another main reason that discipline in private schools is better is because suspension or expulsion is the end. The student is notified along with his parents and literally the case is closed. The only exceptions would be if the private school is bound by a federal program, i.e., special education, or has a written contract with parents stating a child is entitled to a hearing upon receiving notice of a suspension or expulsion. Not so in the public schools. An informal hearing is required if a student challenges his suspension. Also, a hearing in an expulsion case is required, and many times the phrase "I have my rights" is carried to the extreme by our judicial system.

In my opinion, many hearing officers and judges are much too lenient in their handling of student expulsion cases in the public school sector. They permit violent, disruptive students to return to school where they continue their destructive pattern of behavior. My belief is that, when a student comes before the court, their disruptive behavior must have been severe or the case wouldn't have been heard at this level in the first place. Therefore, sending such a student back to his school certainly is not in the best interest of the school or student. The goal is to change the student's behavior. The choice should be made by those charged with the responsibility of deciding what is best for disruptive youths to review the following procedures:

1. Require placement in alternative educational programs apart from the normal school setting that requires no breaking of the rules. Once a rule is broken, out the student goes. Once behavior is judged to be satisfactory, a student may return to his regular school or can continue to complete his education at the alternative school.
2. Place in a limited penal institution strictly for older adolescent students where work, mental and physical discipline are the requirements until such time the student is judged to be able to return to his regular school.
3. Require placement in city or county work programs that require supervision and hard work.
4. Make the parents/guardians responsible for their child's behavior by refusing to admit him back into school until such time the school judges the student is capable of returning.
5. Employ a competent (school oriented) psychiatrist (M.D.) to train teachers in the use of effective techniques related to dealing with disruptive youths and provide counseling assistance to teachers and students.

Public schools cannot continue to be the dumping ground for disruptive students. Disruptive students cannot be allowed to undermine the educational environment for the majority of students who come to school desiring an education.

Let's look back to the crucial question: Who is

offering a better overall education program - private
or public schools? What criteria can parents use in
judging what will be best for their child? What
environment will best prepare their child to be a
contributing member of society?

Spending more money on education in School (A)
over School (B) does not necessarily mean education
becomes better. In my travels I have seen "old"
vintage school buildings with reduced average-per-pupil
expenditures offer an educational package that make
many educators and parents envious. Why? Because,
such schools have chosen to follow the <u>Effective
Schools Research Model</u>, a program well-known to all
educators. Anyone visiting such a school will find the
following:

    (1)   There is leadership at the top
          (Principal).
    (2)   The school environment is conducive
          to learning and instructional
          priorities are addressed.
    (3)   Students are experiencing success
          in their classes.
    (4)   Expectations are established for
          teachers and students.
    (5)   Programs and staff are consistently
          evaluated.

Also, additional research done at Michigan State
University reveals that teachers who are following the
<u>Effective Schools Research Model</u> have the following
beliefs:

    •   Teachers believe that all students
        can learn.
    •   Teachers believe they should teach
        all students.
    •   Teachers believe in setting goals.
    •   Teachers believe they should follow
        school policies and procedures.
    •   Teachers believe they should be
        held accountable.

Looking at the above beliefs, I am reminded of one
private school, the Thornwell School in Clinton, South

Carolina. Supported by the Presbyterian Church, the Thornwell School offers a K-12 program to single-parent children as well as children without parents. Based on my visits and conversations with students and staff, I know the principal operates a school that works because he follows the practices and procedures mentioned above. Upon entering the school, an observer immediately can sense that good things are occurring. Teachers are enthusiastic; there is no yelling at students and no evidence that teachers are passing the time by grading papers, etc. while students sit passively in their seats. The principal is up and around the building, always visible to the staff and making sure things are working. These positive happenings are taking place in a school despite a limited budget with outdated facilities.

On the other hand, I have observed plush, sprawling, affluent public suburban schools that were "urban jungles" in disguise. I have seen private schools, catering to low income families, operating a sound educational program primarily because education was the number one priority. I have seen other affluent private schools with such inferior teaching and leadership that it made me question their existence.

All schools, private or public, have a mission which is offering quality education to the students. This mission differs from school to school, public to public, private to private, and private to public. The difference is determined on what is being done to educate the children. The students who enter school doors in August and September of each year for 175-180 days put their future into the hands of "professionals" called school teachers and school administrators who are employed to train and prepare them for what lies ahead.

Private education certainly has a place in this country. Parents should be given a choice as to what educational setting they prefer for their children, but I strongly suggest the choice must be based on the quality of the final product. Schools are only as good as the teachers and administrators who staff the building. The best equipment and well-constructed school building will not guarantee a child will be

"It's not the teachers
you dismiss that cause
you the problems, it's
the ones you should and
don't dismiss that
cause you problems!"

better educated or taught properly. It is the professionals inside the building that will determine the amount of learning taking place.

Like public education, private education has not been immune to the financial crunch, and many of the good ones have had to close their doors. Private education must rely primarily on tuition and endowments; therefore, such schools must consistently market their product in order to keep from going under.

It is interesting to note that even public schools in some of the remote areas of our country are facing closings as well. In Canova, South Dakota, several years ago, the students of Canova High School were facing the closing of their school because the South Dakota law states any school district with less than 35 students faces the loss of state aid. According to a nine-year enrollment projection study, the enrollment would remain at 30. The town at the time had just 194 residents, down from the 1960 census of 247, plus a post office, hardware store, cafe, meat locker, and grocery store. Students at Canova High School decided to take things in their own hands to prevent their school from closing. Through anonymous donations totaling $1,000.00, students ran ads in various papers throughout the country offering one month of free labor to any business willing to move to the area. At the time, no business had decided to move to the school district in eastern South Dakota's farm country about 40 miles northwest of Sioux Falls. An Iowa firm did give the students 100 business cards, and a Canova resident offered $10,000 to any company that would move into the area, and a national moving firm stated it would offer a 20 percent discount to any company or individual moving to Canova. The high school's teachers had recommended that unless enrollment increased it would be in the students' best interests if the district paid their tuition to attend another high school. The school board then voted to keep the school open on a yearly review basis.

So, even our public schools are faced with declining enrollments and closings. In Iowa, the move is on to combine rural public school districts and share a superintendent between districts. This idea met with stiff resistance from one farm school district whose superintendent of schools also served as the basketball coach at the local high school and had won the state basketball championship in 1987. The board of education and community refused to go along with sharing their superintendent with their neighbors. Nothing becomes harder on a superintendent and causes him to age faster than being involved in a school closing.

Another point of interest, when one looks at private vs. public education in this country, is the impact educational fads and movements have had on schools. Over the years, the educational community has been extremely gullible in accepting instructional packages generated by college and university professors, special interest groups or educational divisions of major corporations. Such movements as modern math, individualized instruction, team teaching, metric measurement,   course   electives,   and   now   computer instruction have all spent their time on the elementary and secondary scenes of public and private education. Only two fads introduced years ago are still with us today in both private and public schools: psychological testing (over-used) and the Carnegie units. (Advocates of restructuring believe a measurement of competency would be more valid than measurement of seat time.)

This is not to imply that all of the movements were without benefit because they all had their unique contributions to the educational community.   However, many school systems bought packaged ideas "lock, stock, and barrel" spending money on untested ideas. Many a public school superintendent made the mistake of converting a school district entirely over to a "movement" and labeled it as "educational advancement." But to others, especially the instructional staff, it was a different story. Teachers were not prepared to accept universal administrative mandates requiring conversion to new programs of instruction. Many of these innovations failed and with them went many a superintendent. Some school administrators are anxious to join bandwagons hoping it will create a "lighthouse" district or school which will make them look better in the eyes of the board of education and community. What they fail to realize is that any movement, if it is to be implemented with success, must be evaluated and implemented with patience and proper training.

Comparing private education to public education in adopting educational fads and movements, we find private education in general has fared better than public education. There has been generally more stability in sticking to the 3 R's in our private schools. This does not mean that private schools have not bought into educational fads and movements, but they have done so with more selectivity than public schools. In some cases, private schools have laid back and waited to see the outcome of happenings and results in their neighboring public schools before they ventured into the area of change. Such a process has preserved their credibility and has been one of the factors that has made private education attractive and appealing over the years. Private educators take pride in telling the educational community they have consistently maintained a solid educational program for students over the years and have not been taken in by educational fads and movements. Private schools have, nevertheless, been subject to criticism because of a lack of innovativeness; but they counter with maintaining student discipline, small class size and increasing student achievement scores. However, the term <u>K-12 private education</u> is not automatically synonymous with quality.

With all that has been said about private vs. public education, let's conclude with some remarks about the title of this chapter, "Your Choice: Private or Public Education?"

I trust by now I have made the point that both private and public schools have their advantages and disadvantages. I trust also that I have made the point that private schools, in general, present to the public a better image as one looks at student achievement scores, and that better student discipline usually prevails within the hallways of most private elementary and secondary schools. However, I also indicated there are many excellent public schools in this country. They are excellent because they are working, and they are working because they are turning out a quality product known as education. Although I have been narrow in citing examples, please understand that to try to list all of the successful public schools in this country with which I am familiar, is a dangerous process to undertake for fear of leaving some good ones out. Besides, the criteria for judging is general and, therefore, subject to interpretation. But, public education is not as bad as many private critics claim it to be. Step inside a public school district and find out for yourself: Observe, listen, ask questions, and then form your opinions. Look at news releases, observe classrooms, and talk to teachers, custodians, secretaries, cooks; they are the front-line people in any school building, be it private or public. Caring for children, planning for the future, striving for quality, and gaining community support become the trademarks of producing quality schools. Once again the thing to keep in mind in any comparison of private vs. public education is that East Overshoe High School with all of its unique characteristics must be stacked up against others like East Overshoe High School across our country before one can really find out if the school or schools are producing as they should.

I can tell you this, my choice as to whether I would send my child to a K-12 public or private school, would be an easy one if in my search I would come across a school or school system that, in addition to the requirements previously mentioned, would have the following practices in place:

1. Teachers were not bound by the tenure laws;
2. The media center was staffed with a competent librarian who taught demonstration lessons to teachers, directed the creative construction of learning materials, in addition to assuming the present-day duties of primarily cataloging books and periodicals;
3. Guidance counselors were found to be part of the administrative team working side-by-side with assistant principals in maintaining discipline in addition to their counseling and career planning

"Teachers prefer to work in schools where goals are set and communicated."

endeavors;
4. Meetings were judged by the faculty
    to be highly productive, unique and
    motivating;
5. Teachers who excelled were awarded
    additional incentives;
6. Principal's evaluation was based
    on merit utilizing individual
    goal-setting formats;
7. Evidence of strong community
    support was present;
8. Evidence of on-going staff
    development programs and
    professional growth was found;
9. Student perceptions of teachers
    were positive.

Provided these practices are in place, a parent can rest assured that any school will yield positive educational outcomes, be it public or private. However, I realize such practices are not found totally in our public or private elementary and secondary schools. It makes little sense to spend millions of dollars on positions (public/private) that have little effect towards achieving desired outcomes. Librarians and guidance counselors, for example, need to dive into the water of accountability and swim with their teacher and administrator colleagues. It is imperative for school administrators to require action-oriented performance rather than passive-oriented performance from their support personnel in both public and private K-12 schools in this country. The total staff in a school must be held accountable, and for some it will require a major overhaul of their job responsibilities.

If the main priorities of parents in selecting an education for their children are student discipline, moral training, individual attention, less threat of work stoppages, and a somewhat better chance of a son or daughter entering college, then the choice could be private education. On the other hand, if parents desire expanded extra-curricular activities, vocational subjects, expanded curriculum and programs, veteran teachers and administrators, a more pluralistic student environment (heterogeneous), and a good chance of a son or daughter entering college, then the choice could be public education. It's the parents' responsibility to choose the best educational environment for their child by visiting schools (both private and public), asking questions related to the issues discussed so far, and then comparing the answers to the individual needs and abilities of their own child.

Education in this country, especially at our elementary and secondary levels, must continue to improve if our country is going to move forward with a vision and hope. All forms of education, private and public, must strive to offer the best educational product possible through professional initiative and competition. Public and private education, in my judgement, must survive based on their own merits. When parents can choose public or private education for their children, then the pressure will be on both sectors to produce.

Solid roots in education will be established when private and public schools join together to address the challenges of education in the 21st century. There is a need for both elementary and secondary public and private education in this country. Educational excellence can be achieved in any type of schooling, provided the paid professionals are doing their job. When the job is getting done, then our total society benefits.

Chapter 9

The Curriculum: Where Is It Heading?

"...diploma requirements which are stated in terms of courses completed rather than outcomes reached may have little bearing on the actual learning achievements of students."

--American Association of
School Administrators
taken from <u>Challenges for
School Leaders</u>

There are two main definitions of <u>curriculum</u>. One refers to everything that happens in the school; the other refers to what is to be taught and how it will be taught. I will address the how and the what.

The purpose of curriculum development in our schools is to assist students and teachers in achieving desired learning outcomes. These outcomes involve acquisition, application and mastery. Ralph Tyler, a household name in education especially in the areas of curriculum and supervision, recommended a model for schools to follow in curriculum development years ago. This model answered the following questions:

1. What educational purposes should the school seek to attain?
2. What educational experiences can be provided that are likely to attain these purposes?
3. How can these educational experiences be effectively organized?
4. How can we determine whether these purposes are being attained? (Kimbrough and Nunnery)

School administrators today, at all levels of education, should ask themselves Tyler's four-question approach. The approach is practical and easily understood.

Question 1, involving educational purposes, starts with goal formation. Teachers have to know what the goals of the school are. Many of our public schools in this country are functioning under drifting management. Without established educational goals, two things will usually occur when passing "fads" in education are seized by some teachers and presented to administrators. One, the idea will be rejected or put on the back burner; or two, it will be accepted and implemented without any careful thought or consideration given to whether the program is needed or if it will work. If implemented, the program will usually be heralded by administrators as a step forward in advancing public education. No program development or implementation should take place within a public school or school system unless (1) goals have been formulated based on a review of an assortment of qualitative and quantitative data and (2) the program is consistent with the stated goals of the school or school district. Once on board with stated goals, curriculum developers in our schools and school districts must choose to convert the goals into meaningful and attainable programs.

Question 2, offered by Tyler, deals with the way the subject matter is to be taught. Here we have a problem because of the many conflicting views formulated by "experts" on how students learn. Some say students learn more if the teacher interacts in a more non-structured environment. Others say the direct approach is better--lecturing and regularly testing; others say the way students learn is through direct involvement and application. The guiding concept in teaching a subject must relate to how individual children learn. No two children or adults are alike, so the thrust of curriculum development in our schools must focus on diagnosing to determine the dominant learning style of the learner and then present a curriculum package that offers flexibility to the teacher to teach the subject utilizing various methods of instruction.

Question 3 relates to grade level organization for purposes of instruction. Probably no other country has as many variations for grouping students for purposes of instruction as the United States. From grade organizations (such as K-6, 5-8, 7-12, 7-8-9, 10-11-12, and non-graded, coupled with modular and standard scheduling practices), one finds a constant redesigning of grade levels. Declining or increasing enrollment may bring about grade level changes in certain school systems on an annual basis. There is ability grouping based on student achievement in certain subject areas including, but not limited to, reading, science, math, and vocational subjects and non-ability grouping in others where students from a wide range of ability levels are brought together without using a stated criteria.

Question 4 relates to evaluating whether or not desired outcomes are being achieved. Is the curriculum within a given subject achieving what it is suppose to achieve? Is the content applicable to the needs of students and are they learning? Based on the school district's achievement goals, are the basic skills being mastered? The answers to these questions require ongoing evaluation. If the process of evaluation involving interviews, questionnaires, reviewing objective data and observation reveals shortcomings then the school curriculum people must find out why and make the necessary corrections or changes. The most important choice is to review and act. Too many of our educational programs in our public schools are never evaluated to determine if they are achieving desired outcomes.

As school administrators and teachers respond to Tyler's four key questions in pursuing meaningful curriculum development, the bottom line is twofold: (1) What subjects are to be taught? (2) Should more time be allotted for teaching the basic subjects vs. non-basic subjects?

For years in this country, public education has been the scapegoat for the ills of our society, especially during the last decade. Public schools are expected to handle the problems that are no longer being handled by the home or the church. Schools are pressured to teach classes about environmental decay,

AIDS and other communicable health problems and deal
with family breakups, poverty, and a rising teenage
pregnancy rate. On the other hand, school personnel
have been told that the primary mission of curriculum
development in our public schools must center around
the development and teaching of the "basics."

Children must be taught to read, write, and
compute. States have responded to both demands by
mandating curriculum reforms and revisions such as expanding graduation credits; improving the content areas
of science, mathematics, English and social studies;
extending the school day and year; and providing pre-
kindergarten programs, plus reducing class size in
various subject areas. According to Education Week
(6 February 1985), curriculum reform has occurred in
about 90 percent of the states. I am convinced that,
with an ever-changing society and the corresponding
knowledge demands put on our public schools by such
changes, the choice must be made by state departments
of education to require local school systems to teach
the basics. If the requirement is not enforced, attempting to turn out an educated student majority will
become a thing of the past. Schools cannot continue to
add another niche in the curriculum every time a problem occurs in our present-day society, as evidenced
through state-mandated special programs. Many of our
urban schools are frustrated trying to teach the basics
on one hand so students achieve respectable scores on
state/district achievement tests while, at the same
time, attempting to work a complete liberal arts/social
issues curriculum into the daily schedule. Public
education in this country has always been the servant
to our larger society, but what is occurring is that
the landlord has been putting too many demands on the
servant.

Present-day practices in curriculum development
must be revamped to cope with the demanding times of a
fast-approaching new century of living. We must teach
the basic subjects in our public schools during the
allotted school hours. This must become the number one
priority in curriculum development. The basics have
never left our public school systems in this country,
but instructional time devoted to teaching them is
becoming shorter and shorter. The reason is obvious.

Demands from outside support groups, as well as state and federal agencies, have mandated special programs be taught to students on a regular basis which cuts into the teaching time allocated for teaching the basics.

At one time in this country, the basics were taught from 8 a.m. until 4 p.m. Everything else that went on was done after 4 p.m. Today, not only is the school day shortened, but attempts to teach the basics have become fragmented with pull-out programs such as gifted, bilingual, and remedial instruction, in addition to special assemblies and non-basic courses that have been added to the schedule.

The curriculum in any public school should be aimed at (1) dropout prevention, (2) use of modern instructional technology, and (3) vocational preparation, all interwoven and related to the basic subject areas. Within any public school system, certain percentages of graduating students go on to four-year colleges/universities, technical colleges, the military, as well as the general work force. Knowing this as a fact, the curriculum in a school district must reflect the requirements, and knowledge base must be related to these post-secondary areas.

Therefore, in building a schedule of courses and sections to be taught within a given school year, courses must be offered with content which relates directly to the basic subject areas. Once this is done, any additional time left over within the school day can be used to offer non-basic subjects with the exception being physical education/health. Students need to be directed towards maintaining a sound physical body. Therefore, a physical education/health curriculum should be offered that is developmental for K-12 and incorporates fitness, sportsmanship in individual as well as group competition, nutrition, drug prevention, and sex education. With a minimum of twice a week at every grade, students need proper physical exercise. Developmental exercise should become a requirement for every student, every week up through and including the time they graduate from high school. The old adage that a sound mind and body facilitates learning is certainly applicable to today's youth. Characteristic of the lifestyle of an increasing number

"Learning cannot be
forced upon a child."

of young people attending our present-day public schools is lack of proper exercise and rest, over-indulging in the consumption of junk food, and drug addiction. Dr. Wynn F. Updyke, director of the Chrysler Fund AAU testing program, conducted a 10-year lifestyle study of 6- to 17-year-olds. Dr. Updyke stated: "The best investment parents can make in the physical fitness of their children is to insist on high quality physical education programs in their schools" (Vejnoska, "Youngsters Are Getting Fatter, Not Fitter," USA Today). Overall, the study concluded today's youngsters are getting fatter, not fitter. The physical education/health program that incorporates in the curriculum developmental exercise and health components will serve a vital role to our youth and country. There is an abundance of research and evidence that reveals a positive correlation between achievement and proper exercise. Requiring physical exercise for every student at all grade levels must become an instructional requirement along with teaching the basics.

Back to the "basics," William J. Bennett, in his closing days as United States Secretary of Education, announced his famous James Madison Elementary School curriculum. What Mr. Bennett proposed in his report was the strengthening of the curriculum in kindergarten through the eighth grades as illustrated in Figure 1, and includes emphasis on developing the student around basic learning requirements.

This author endorses the Bennett proposal providing two important issues are addressed: (1) All subjects must be geared to the ability level of the student. For example, Bennett's proposal suggests all 8th graders should have physics and chemistry. I maintain that unless these subjects are taught at the level the students can understand and apply, we will add more students to the "at-risk" list. Teaching the basic subjects must be based on ability grouping, and then must be delivered to students by breaking the subject down into small chunks. As each chunk of information or skill is mastered, the teacher must immediately provide positive reinforcement and move on to the next block of learning. (2) From 7th through the 12th grades, vocational instruction must be part of the curriculum as it applies to the basics. For exam-

FIGURE 1.

The Program in Brief: A Plan for Kindergarten through Grade 8

SUBJECT	KINDERGARTEN THROUGH GRADE 3	GRADES 4 THROUGH 6	GRADES 7 AND 8
ENGLISH	INTRODUCTION TO READING AND WRITING	INTRODUCTION TO CRITICAL READING	Grade 7: SURVEY OF ELEMENTARY GRAMMAR AND COMPOSITION Grade 8: SURVEY OF ELEMENTARY LITERARY ANALYSIS
SOCIAL STUDIES	INTRODUCTION TO HISTORY, GEOGRAPHY, AND CIVICS	Grade 4: U.S. HISTORY TO CIVIL WAR Grade 5: U.S. HISTORY SINCE 1865 Grade 6: WORLD HISTORY TO THE MIDDLE AGES	Grade 7: WORLD HISTORY FROM THE MIDDLE AGES TO 1900 Grade 8: WORLD GEOGRAPHY and U.S. CONSTITUTIONAL GOVERNMENT
MATHEMATICS	INTRODUCTION TO MATHEMATICS	INTERMEDIATE ARITHMETIC AND GEOMETRY	*Two from among the following one-year courses:* GENERAL MATH; PRE-ALGEBRA and ALGEBRA
SCIENCE	INTRODUCTION TO SCIENCE	Grade 4: EARTH SCIENCE AND OTHER TOPICS Grade 5: LIFE SCIENCE AND OTHER TOPICS Grade 6: PHYSICAL SCIENCE AND OTHER TOPICS	Grade 7: BIOLOGY Grade 8: CHEMISTRY AND PHYSICS
FOREIGN LANGUAGE	[OPTIONAL]	INTRODUCTION TO FORMAL LANGUAGE	FORMAL LANGUAGE STUDY *Two years strongly recommended*
FINE ARTS	MUSIC AND VISUAL ART	MUSIC AND VISUAL ART	MUSIC APPRECIATION and ART APPRECIATION *One semester of each required*
PHYSICAL EDUCATION/ HEALTH	PHYSICAL EDUCATION AND HEALTH	PHYSICAL EDUCATION AND HEALTH	PHYSICAL EDUCATION AND HEALTH

Source: Bennett, William J. James Madison Elementary School: A Curriculum for American Students. United States Department of Education, August 1988.

ple, students not only learn geometry, but they learn how to use that knowledge in a woodworking shop or how to use math in personal financial management. In a recent speech, Alfred E. Gray, Commandant of the United States Marine Corps, told a group of school administrators in South Carolina that the number one discipline problem with marine recruits on Okinawa and Japan was that they couldn't balance a checkbook. The grounding in basic curriculum and related subjects determine whether the educational foundation is solid or weak in public schools. Constantly adding a proliferation of unrelated courses to the curriculum weakens the educational foundation of any school.

For example, this author is opposed to bilingual education. Simply stated, students who enter our public schools should learn to speak English, not be pulled out of the regular scheduled day for special instruction in their native language in order to learn English. This has never made sense to me, even though I have been involved directly with bilingual education when I served as superintendent of schools. Research findings concerning the effect of bilingual instruction and the ability of students to learn English are inconclusive. There are many Japanese schools that have been established after school and on Saturdays across this country. The students learn about their own traditions, culture, and language away from the traditional American school structure.

Driver education should not be offered (instructional as well as driving time) until after the regular school day and should involve maximum time behind the wheel.

Music, art, drama should continue to be offered as electives at the high school level, but only on the basis that students have fulfilled their commitment to understanding the basics.

Gifted "pull out" programs at the elementary and secondary levels should not, in this author's mind, be a part of the daily program. Gifted education sounds great to parents who have children in the program; however, some questions need to be asked. Are they really learning or achieving what they are supposed to be learning or achieving based on qualitative and quantitative evidence? Pulling certain students away from their regular classroom and sending them down the hall once or twice a week to receive "gifted instruc- tion" is unnecessary. Provided with added support for the regular classroom teacher, such students could stay within the confines of the regular classroom and re- ceive an instructional program that has been geared to their individual interest and ability levels. Parents who have children in a gifted program need to ask themselves, "Is the program working for my child, and is it achieving desired outcomes?"

Foreign languages should be offered as electives, along with the fine arts, to students starting at grade nine. The need to learn a foreign language is impor- tant in today's world of global travel and dialogue, but once again this author's position is that educators must first choose to teach basic subject content at the elementary level and expand that content to every student at the secondary level. When corporate execu- tives and higher education officials say repeatedly that there is a critical need in this country to have our youth better prepared in the basics, then it's time that the issue be addressed and acted upon in all of our elementary and secondary schools.

When we talk about expanding the curriculum for advanced study at the high school level, we should first talk about expanding it in English (including communication skills), math, social studies (including economics and psychology), science, computer science, vocational education and physical/health education.

When we look at reducing the curriculum to make room for basic subject courses, including advance offerings, we should take a look at removing bilingual education, fine arts (elective only), driver education (after school), gifted education, foreign language (elective only), plus any other course offering that is not directly related to the basic subject areas.

A liberal arts/humanities curriculum should be taught within the structure of the basic curriculum. For an example, when students are studying the War between the States, they would also learn the music of the time, the poems, the stories, the art, and what was occurring globally. We must have an interdisciplinary approach to teaching the basics especially at the high school level.

The choice to teach the basics usually will find support among front line educators; however, where the choice gets sidetracked is over time. Many school administrators will say there just isn't enough time in an 8 a.m. to 3 p.m. school day to offer what needs to be offered. This is true in many secondary schools throughout the country. After-school employment is a necessity for many students. The need for students to have additional income to help a single parent is as real for their survival as it is for a husband or wife earning joint incomes in order to maintain a household. From the streets of Chicago and Los Angeles to the farmlands of North Dakota and West Texas, the need to work and leave school early is a fact. This is the only way many students can ever hope to further their education either at a technical school or college.

Addressing this student need will require a bold new look at how we are presently running our schools. Instead of the usual 8 a.m. to 3 p.m. schedule, schools should be open the year round and the school day should be extended. Not only will that create more time to teach the curriculum, but it will give a built-in flexibility factor that permits students who need to work to have an extended amount of time off (more than three months each summer) each year during their high school years to be employed on a full-time daily basis. Students would have extended time to learn a vocation and also have more time each year to observe what is required of them in the "real" world. Teachers employed in a year-round school program, for example, would have the choice regarding the time they would be on board to teach daily and the time they wanted off based on a twelve-month quarter system - three quarters on, one quarter off, etc.

Another choice that should be made regarding the issue of having enough time in a school day to offer the curriculum is to open schools up earlier and close them later. For example, starting a school day at 6 a.m. and keeping the doors open to 7 p.m. has special

"If you want kids
to achieve,
link them up
with achievers."

significance, especially at the elementary and middle
school levels. Parents could drop their children off
on their way to work knowing that they are safely at
school under proper supervision and guidance before and
after school. Under such a program, former latch-key
children (previously discussed in chapter 7) would no
longer be left at home unattended. Teachers who volunteered would be paid extra and would not only supervise
the children before and after school hours but might
offer remedial instruction to those youngsters who need
help in the various curriculum areas. See Chapter 7
for a list of other before and after school learning
options taught by teachers, volunteers, those in business, and retirees which could also be repeated later
in the evening for adults, i.e., adult literacy
tutoring.

It seems to this author that such a choice of
extending the traditional 8 a.m. to 3 p.m. daily
schedule to one of 6 a.m. to 7 p.m., combined with
schools being open the year round, would better serve
students, parents, professional staff and the community
at-large. For one thing, closing schools three to four
months out of every year is not a fiscally responsible
way to run the important business of public education.
The stockholders of each local school system in this
country need to know the facts about the importance and
the reasoning behind the extended day and keeping
schools open year round.

Once the decision has been made to teach the
curriculum of basics, utilizing the concept of
year-round schools and extending the normal school day,
the next set of choices evolves around the development
of what is called curriculum guides.

The curriculum guides that teachers follow in
teaching a skill or topic to students at the elementary
and secondary levels in our public schools serve as the
skeletal framework for each subject area, supposedly
providing outlines, guidelines and projected outcomes.
Key questions addressed in curriculum guide development
are as follows:

> 1. How will the content be determined
>   for each subject area?

2. How does the curriculum guide
    relate to the district's long-
    range plan?
3. Is there a "check up" to determine
    if there is reinforcement of
    content and skills in the higher
    grades?
4. What is being done to update the
    content in each subject area and is
    it supplemental?
5. How extensive are the existing
    curriculum guides being used by
    teachers?
6. Do basic subject curriculum guides
    offer instructional strategies
    relating to the different ways
    students learn (auditory,
    kinesthetic and visually)?
7. Are the curriculum guides
    sequentially developed in subject
    matter so that the majority of
    students obtain 90-95% mastery?

Unfortunately, in some schools the answers to the
preceding questions are as follows:

1. They are not used.
2. Skills/content and teaching
    strategies within subject area
    need updating.
3. Evaluation procedures are lacking.
4. Textbooks are being substituted and
    used as curriculum guides.
5. Following curriculum guide
    instructional procedures vary from
    school to school within a district.
6. School board policies relating to
    overall curriculum development are
    weak or non-existent.
7. Children are not always tested
    through standardized testing
    on the level taught.

Designing curriculum guides around the requirements to improve accountability in content development
could be dealt with by incorporating the following

procedures.

First, begin by surveying local area businesses such as department stores, restaurants, gas stations, etc. asking for feedback regarding the ability of employed students to effectively compute, speak, and write in an acceptable manner. Also, request recommendations from these employers on additional skills/content that they feel should be included in curriculum guides at the elementary/secondary levels.

Second, repeat the same process as stated above except that inquiries should be directed to various two- and four-year higher educational institutions where most students from local area schools attend.

Third, seek teacher input at all levels.

Fourth, send questionnaires to the school district's college students in order to discover academic skill areas in which they feel inadequately prepared.

Fifth, review national trends regarding suggested skills to be taught at elementary and secondary levels.

Sixth, once the information is received from steps 1 and 2, bring together teachers and competent curriculum-oriented administrators to design a format that includes the following headings within each subject and corresponding grade level:

    a. Area/level,
    b. Materials and supplies to be used,
    c. Suggested teaching activities and
        alternatives,
    d. Performance objectives, and
    e. Evaluation procedures.

Seventh, review all curriculum guides every two to three years to make sure they are up to date with the changing times and are sequential in skill and content development.

The concern over the lack of accountability in curriculum development in our public schools has recently generated a movement by a panel of state board members who are recommending the removal of the Carnegie Unit System from our public schools. Students over the years have gained credits towards graduation by taking a minimum prescribed number of high school courses (i.e., four units of English, two units of math, etc.) within the basic subject areas. To graduate from most high schools in this country requires anywhere from 18 to 22 units of course work.

The panel has suggested replacing the unit system with a central core of courses within the general areas of foreign language, health, language arts, mathematics, physical education, science and the fine arts. What is being proposed is that state boards of education establish performance objectives within the seven major areas of the curriculum as stated above and then hold local schools accountable for meeting such standards. How each school district would go about meeting the performance objectives would be a local option (Rothman, Education Week, 2 November 1988, p. 1). For example, the selection of textbooks, testing procedures, class scheduling, and teaching practices could become the responsibility of each local school system, and not the state, since the responsibility of meeting state-designated curriculum outcomes would be turned over to local school districts.

The thought of going from the Carnegie Unit System to a proposed core curriculum, with stated performance standards, is worth noting. It makes sense because such a choice would involve the much-needed overhauling of teacher certification standards. It would require effective teaching and increase decision-making at the local level which, in my opinion, is the only way we can expect major reforms to occur in public education.

Once the subjects are decided upon, daily and yearly schedules would be in place, and corresponding curriculum guides would be developed and distributed through inservice programs. Then it would become the responsibility of competent administrators and teachers working and planning together to make sure the curriculums in our schools would "come alive" with motivating, productive, and unique teaching procedures. The process called teaching produces the results once the curriculum and teaching schedules are in place. Content matter is dead weight in any school or school district unless teachers resurrect the content through effective teaching techniques thus creating in students a desire to learn. The best curriculum designs in the world are worthless unless effective teaching methods are used to move the subject matter into the eager, waiting minds of students.

Our children can learn what they need to learn, but it will not happen by chance. Subjects must be taught effectively and creatively. Less reliance must be placed on commercially prepared ditto masters and more time spent working with individual student's problems. Sterile workbook activities must be replaced by creative teaching techniques. Anyone can pass out seat work. Good teachers know how to teach and motivate.

Progress in student achievement can be forthcoming by (1) determining what is to be taught and when and (2) teaching it effectively by applying the principles of how people learn.

To make learning stick in the minds of students requires a classroom setting where the number one priority is effective teaching. Whether students become "turned on" to learning or not can often be judged by what happens when the bell rings signaling the end of class. Instead of rushing out of classrooms like they have been shot out of a cannon, students who are "turned on" to learning hang around the teacher's desk, questioning, probing and reflecting over the events of the last forty-five minutes. When this happens day in and day out in any classroom, the curriculum is being delivered to students in an effective, stimulating, and thought-provoking manner.

All public schools under the direction of assertive and effective leadership should be able to increase test scores regardless of location or resources. Administrators and teachers in any school district determine whether students learn or don't learn. Educators who offer excuses for low test scores are simply refusing to take responsibility for their students. There are too many examples today of schools and individual teachers making significant progress in the face of overwhelming odds.

"School personnel
respect school
administrators who
are decision makers."

Once the curriculum is developed and in place, there should be 90% to 95% mastery on the part of the individual students if the knowledge base is taught effectively. In too many schools, the percent of mastery is far below this percentage. To achieve such a rate involves finding individual mastery levels for each child in various subject areas and then embarking upon an organized plan of effective teaching. Grouping for instruction is a major factor in determining student learning. Research from the American Association of Supervision and Curriculum Development (A.S.C.D.) reveals that subjects requiring basic skill instruction is most effectively taught when there is ability grouping, utilizing the self-paced approach. This is especially true in the teaching of math and reading. Concept instruction, on the other hand, is most effectively taught in non-ability grouping patterns. The teacher's role is that of a resource person. Whether teaching basic skills or concepts, there is one key principle that must be followed by all teachers. That principle is simply to incorporate the "success model of teaching." Whether a student makes a small gain or large gain, he must be encouraged to press on. Too many gold stars are passed out in classrooms to students who routinely get all the answers correct and not to those who are giving it their best shot. The way you get the F-student to become a D-student and then a C-student and hopefully an A-producer is to reward the young mind with positive reinforcement along the way. Failure breeds more failure. Success breeds success.

I'm always leery when I hear teachers, especially college professors, informing students that a test was graded on a curve. It is my belief that if the curriculum is taught effectively, there is little justification for curve grading. There is also no justification for a teacher increasing anxiety in students by stating "I never give A's." There is absolutely nothing wrong in "teaching for the test" if the test lines up with the curriculum. Our goal for student evaluation should be to encourage students, not undermine them. It is a fact that some blocks of content are more difficult than others and require more teaching time. However, in many elementary, secondary, as well as post-secondary classrooms in this country, teachers must run races

to see how rapidly they can cover subject matter.
Students become out-distanced by their teachers. Many
give up in despair knowing that they will never catch
up and will never pass the next test. Some teachers
believe it is a sign of weakness to spend additional
time with various students to make certain they are
within range of whatever is being taught. Nothing
could be further from the truth. Assessing mastery
levels of students on a continuous basis and subsequently adjusting the teaching and testing pace to
correspond to such various levels is a sign of effective and caring teaching.

Administrators and teachers must choose to establish and offer an ambitious curriculum filled with
teaching strategies and expectations and then use it in
the same fashion as an athletic team uses their playbook. Coaches and players follow a playbook. If
things don't work, the playbook is revised based on the
abilities of the players as well as what is known about
the upcoming opponent. The important fact is: The
playbook is used, not thrown in some locker where no
one can find it! Everyone, teachers and students
alike, must become tuned in to the "plan" as a team.
Teachers must see themselves as coaches taking their
class to victory, not as adversaries trying to see how
difficult they can make it for the class to succeed.

When the whole class works toward a common goal,
the following results occur:

        1.   Student attendance increases,
        2.   Test scores and student enthusiasm
             soars,
        3.   Community support increases,
        4.   Dropout rates lower,
        5.   Discipline problems decline, and
        6.   School vandalism diminishes.

Most students can learn whatever it is the teacher
wants them to learn, but such a goal will never be
realized unless the curriculum becomes exciting and
productive through meaningful teaching. Curriculum and
teaching are similar to an eighteen-wheeler going down
the interstate. The curriculum is the trailer, full of
content; the teacher with his teaching techniques

"Teachers should always
ask themselves: Would
I like being a student
in my class?"

represents the tractor. The curriculum, regardless of how well designed, will never move learning forward in our schools unless it is hooked up to teachers that can move the contents down the road of learning to the desired destination.

Too many of our curriculum practices are sterile and out of date. For example, what evidence is available supporting the practice that attending the same class for forty-five minutes each day, five days a week, would yield more knowledge to students than meeting three times a week for ninety minutes? Colleges and universities have offered three-credit-hour courses for years; and if it works for higher education, who is to say it wouldn't work at the secondary level for our public schools? It is certainly not the amount of time spent on teaching a skill or topic that determines mastery, but instead how effectively the teacher uses the time alloted to teach whatever is to be taught. There is a good chance that such a choice in scheduling would improve secondary teacher morale by giving teachers more time to plan instead of having back-to-back classes five days a week which is the current practice in the majority of secondary schools throughout the U.S. Such a practice would likely reduce student boredom.

We know that drastic choices must be made to improve curriculum in our public schools. To do so requires two key ingredients: change and evaluation. The need for change in restructuring our curriculum to one of basic offerings within our public schools must be coupled with the concurrent assessment procedures. Successful corporations make changes every day, but such changes are not done simply for the sake of change. Instead, they are based on evaluation and research designs that reveal evidence for change. The end result of such a process yields desired outcomes.

The need to reshape our curriculum in our present-day public schools or to stay with the "comfortable and familiar" is the choice each local school system must face. Deciding to reshape our curriculum will require drastic operational changes. The guidelines given at the beginning of this chapter will assist administrators in making the right choices in improving their curriculum packages. The blueprints required for solid curriculum building in our public schools must be drawn and studied. Curriculum development must include students becoming involved with creativity, imagination and application. Poor test results reflecting minimum competencies dominate our public education scene at the present; and for this reason, we must be careful not to measure our students' progress solely through the use of standardized testing. Standardized tests are needed in our school districts for comparison data at the national, state and local levels. However, assessment of students must also include procedures that involve oral communication, problem solving and analytical application.

For developers of our public education curriculum, the choice is to design each basic subject guide in such a manner that students end up becoming producers as well as dispensers of their own knowledge. Therefore, more emphasis must be placed on why students give wrong answers and not strictly on the fact that wrong answers were given; more emphasis must be placed on requiring effective innovative teaching throughout the year, not once or twice a year when it's evaluation time; and finally, more emphasis must be placed on use of the curriculum. Addressing such issues will give assurance to administrators, teachers, students, parents and the community that the curriculum for any given school district is heading in the right direction.

Chapter 10

What Are The Choices?

*"Revolution is no exaggeration; that's what is
needed to make teaching professional--and to
attract people of professional caliber into our
ranks. The revolution must be dramatic; it must
be now; it must be thorough."*

--Albert Shanker
President, American
Federation of Teachers

This urgent plea from Albert Shanker is echoed by
everyone concerned with the future and quality of
education in this country. Shanker maintains that
revolution in public education must take place in the
areas of salaries, discipline, class size, student/
teacher match and professionalism.

Besides supporting the need for drastic changes in
our public schools, Al Shanker is tough on incompetent
teaching. He realizes that support for his A.F.T.
Union must come through effective membership performance if the goal of achieving membership strength and
influence is to be realized. The President of A.F.T.
wants this goal achieved in every affiliated unionized
school district, and he knows the best bargaining tool
teachers can have at the bargaining table is to take a
stand against teacher incompetency.

In addition to the areas that Mr. Shanker insists
need changing, there is also a tremendous need to revolutionize and overhaul our goals and practices in the
areas of educational administration, school boards,
teaching, education schools, and curriculum.

In 1983 <u>School Board News</u> (30 November 1983) cited eight major reports suggesting needed reforms that must occur if public education is going to improve in this country. Unfortunately, years later, it is still necessary to address the same needs.

1. <u>A Nation at Risk</u> (The National Commission on Excellence in Education).

Highlights:

. Strengthen high school graduation requirements with emphasis in English, mathematics, science, social studies, computer science, foreign language
. Lengthen school year
. Incentives for reducing teacher shortages in key subject areas
. Address the needs of minority students

2. <u>Action for Excellence</u> (Education Commission of the States).

Highlights:

. Improved curriculum
. Periodic tests of achievement administered
. Improvement of teacher certification and better pay with built-in incentives
. Establishment of business partnerships with schools

3. <u>Educating Americans for the 21st Century</u> (The National Science Board, Commission on Precollege Education in Mathematics, Science and Technology).

Highlights:

. More teaching time spent instructing math and science, K-12
. College entrance requirements to include four years of math, four

years of science and one year of
computer science
. Social promotion in the grades
curtailed
. Establishment of a National Education Council and the National
Science Board to advance curriculum
evaluation in the schools
. Local school boards promotion of
partnerships with government and
business and create regional
computer centers for teacher
education

4. **America's Competitive Challenge: The Need for
a National Response** (Business-Higher Education Forum).

Highlights:

. Loans offered to students to attract
engineering students to teaching
careers
. Business world's provision of
equipment and personnel to support
university research and to improve
precollege education

5. **Federal Elementary and Secondary Education
Policy** (The Twentieth Century Fund Task Force).

Highlights:

. A unified core curriculum which
would include the basic skill
subjects plus computer training and
foreign language
. Federal governmental funding of a
master teacher program
. Increased federal funding to improve
math and science education
. Opportunities for public school
students to acquire proficiency in a
second language sponsored by the
federal government and carried out
by state and local school governments

- Fellowship grants to students who
  fail local or state competency tests
  to attend remedial programs

6. <u>Academic Preparation for College - What Students Need to Know and Be Able to Do</u> (The College Board).

Highlights:

- More emphasis on teaching basic
  knowledge of computers
- More emphasis on teaching the
  humanities
- Student proficiency in application
  of basic math principles, use of
  computers and calculators, plus
  knowledge of algebra and geometry
  prior to entering college
- Basic knowledge of at least one area
  of science, such as earth science,
  biology or chemistry plus a factual
  knowledge of politics and economic
  institutions should be attained
  before entering college

7. <u>A Study of Schooling</u> (John Goodlad).

Highlights:

- Children starting school at age 4
- Elementary schools not having
  over 400 students, secondary schools
  600-800, junior highs eliminated
- Local curriculum centers established
  to improve course work, tracking of
  students abolished
- Identifying employees with leadership potential as principals, two-
  year study leaves should be granted
  so potential principals can earn a
  certificate for professional competency

8. <u>High School: A Report on Secondary Schooling in America</u> (The Carnegie Foundation for the Movement of

Teaching).

Highlights:

- Writing instruction in every class
- Improvement of working conditions for teachers
- High school districts having an arrangement with community colleges so dropouts can return part-time or full-time to complete their education
- Business community providing scholarships, field trips, and tutorials for students and cash awards for outstanding teachers, corporate grants to provide sabbaticals for outstanding principals.

A projected cost figure to implement the above recommendations would be in the hundreds of millions. Even if the money were available, what assurance would the taxpayers have that the necessary reform at the local level in their elementary and secondary public schools would occur? The choices made by local tax-payers, the policies set by the local school board, and visionary management that hold persons accountable will determine the quality of education in our public schools.

State departments of education, in conjuction with local school districts, have the power to add or delete courses in schools, extend the length of the school year and day, upgrade teacher certification standards and requirements, implement achievement testing, es-tablish student and school recognition programs, and require accountable evaluation of personnel. We hear much about legal restrictions, which some claim prevent the advancement of education in this country. That just isn't so. It is true, however, that the local school administrators who are supposedly hired to provide administrative leadership have been handicapped by two continuing factors:

1. Lack of local support

"The bottom line is,
America's fight for
long term competitiveness
ultimately will be won
or lost not in the halls
of congress, ... not
in the boardrooms
around the world... but
in America's classrooms."

--John L. Clendenin,
CEO Bell South
Corporation,
Chairman, U.S.
Chamber of Commerce

2. State and federal bureaucracy

Without local support for public education, it is hard to keep things progressing towards educational excellence and reform. When school systems fail to gain local support, educational advancement comes to a standstill; and state and federal departments of education take over, which results in an increasing amount of bureaucratic paperwork as a result of mandates. The paperwork alone demanded by state and federal departments is frustrating. Today more and more time is spent filling out state required forms, preventing teachers from having time to plan and meet with individual students and parents. The reason for state and federal intervention into public education has been twofold: (1) political (candidates seeking a political office will use educational issues as their platform in becoming elected) and (2) lack of leadership at the local school level.

Regardless of all the current attention given to local, state, and federal reforms in public education in this country, regardless of how much money is spent, if our public schools are going to improve, then the choice must be made to **do** just that: improve public education starting first at the local level. Show me an accountable, exciting, challenging school or school district, and I guarantee someone or a team of administrators chose to make things happen by initiating and implementing decisive, goal-oriented priorities that address the ever-changing times in public education.

Robert Levering, Milton Moskowitz, and Michael Katz authored a book, The 100 Best Companies to Work For in America (1983). The authors spent about a year visiting 114 companies in 27 different states. An original list of 350 candidates was narrowed down to 114 based on extensive interviews of friends, relatives, executives, recruiters, management consultants, publishers, etc. trying to determine whether or not a stated company was a good place to work. Although like school districts, each company selected was unique, there were certain common characteristics mentioned in the final "100 Best." Each company selected offered good pay and fringe benefits, and beyond these two characteristics, the following similarities existed between companies:

1. Made people feel part of a team,
2. Established good communications and kept people informed as well as encouraged suggestions and complaints,
3. Created a sense of pride in the products and services provided,
4. Promoted from within when qualified,
5. Allowed employees to share in the profits,
6. Practiced good human relations and strived to reduce the rank between top management and other employees,
7. Devoted attention and resources towards creating a good place to work,
8. Encouraged employees to be active in community,
9. Matched employees savings through matching funds,
10. Tried not to lay-off people without first attempting to place employees in other jobs,
11. Established physical fitness workout centers and created medical programs, and
12. Provided in-service programs to improve management skills, etc. and offered reimbursement of tuition for outside courses.

Many of the above characteristics attributed to the "good companies" can be applied to "good schools" and "good school districts." The list of companies included in the "100 Best" ranged from Sam Walton's Wal-Mart to Delta Airlines to unfamiliar companies to most of us like Moog and Olga. What made these companies tick? According to the authors, the one common chord running through the top companies was leadership - strong, exciting, challenging leadership - leadership that stopped talking and started doing - the kind of leadership needed today in our public schools and school systems throughout the country.

The majority of current educational reforms now on
the scene calling for the improvement of public
education are not action-based; instead, they are
philosophies lacking implementing procedures. For
example, what techniques are required to move the paper
reforms into action results? What techniques are
required to train leaders in our schools of education?
What techniques are required to acquire "motivators" in
our administrative positions?

We do know that public schools that are doing the
job of educating children have the following characteristics:

1. The principal provides an educational climate to enhance learning.
2. The principal sets school goals and
   priorities which are effectively
   communicated to the educational
   community and faculty.
3. The principal sets expectations for
   teachers as well as students.
4. The principal is the driving force
   behind a continuous evaluation of
   staff and programs.

All four characteristics of a good school came out
of the previously mentioned The Effective Schools
Research study of the early 1980's. It's the teachers,
under the leadership of school administrators, that
determine how much the students are learning or not
learning. As we mentioned in Chapter 2, school principals pave the way for either good or bad happenings
in a school, for it is their responsibility to move a
school forward. However, the challenge for the administrative team in each school system is to choose annual
priorities which then must be communicated to the
individual school and school district. Once the vision
is in place, it requires leadership skills to transform
the vision into reality. The entire process requires
team work. Team management means creating an atmosphere where employees are eager to produce. They
become contributors to the daily and future operations
of the organization. Employees, under a team management philosophy, are called upon for input in the
decision-making process and, therefore, feel good about

themselves because they are contributors and not order-takers.

Good management motivates personnel to travel in the same direction. It is up to the leaders to decide and communicate what that direction will be and how they will get there. When there is no direction and no leadership, schools begin to drift off course with no compass to guide them. I have observed individual school districts using fifteen different reading programs, nine different math series and evaluating their teachers in as many ways as there are principals and buildings.

School districts that lack a vision are not being accountable to the taxpayers (stockholders) they serve. There should be a "collegial" staffing structure in place in every school district where staff members acquire a feeling of pride and a willingness to achieve desired outcomes. Once decisions are made and everyone is informed of the expectations, the strong leader must hold the wagon on the trail striving to meet the goals that are set. I recently was told prior to giving a speech in one Northwestern state school system that when the administrators got together in the school district they ended up circling their wagons and began shooting at each other. A school can have all the good intentions in the world of what it wants to do to improve education, but unless the choice is made to turn the intentions into priorities and the priorities into plans and the plans into action consistent with the vision of where the district is going, then meeting after meeting and forming committee after committee won't make a hill of beans. The end-product will be confusion, despair, and conflict.

Educational accountability occurs throughout the school district when everyone understands and is a part of the vision. The students become benefactors simply because they are the recipients of a consistent in-structional system. When school districts test low, state and federal mandates start flowing. A decline in educational accountability and performance at the local level puts pressure on state departments of education to do something, and usually they do something in the form of program mandates.

Businesses are feeling the effect of inadequately prepared high school and college graduates. According to a report in U.S.A. Today (3 February 1989), U.S. corporations spend $25 billion a year teaching their employees skills they should have learned in high school. Some companies even have courses in "good manners." And more companies are voicing frustration at receiving new employees who cannot write memos without grammatical errors. Corporations realize that competent personnel will determine their success in a highly competitive market, not gadgets and machines.

Good school administrators, in choosing to hold fast to their visions, understand it takes courage and they cannot expect problems to take care of themselves. Capable leaders are not afraid of conflict for they know that there must be conflict in order for there to be resolution.

Can Administrators Administrate? Can Teachers Teach? What About School Boards? Who's Teaching Our Teachers? Self-Interest Groups: How Powerful Are They? Where do The Stockholders Fit In? Your Choice: Private or Public Education? The Curriculum: Where Is It Heading? Such questions must be dealt with first and choices made before we can advance down the road heading towards a new century of public education. The challenge continues to be one of choice, either to support and get behind the building of quality public education in this country so that the students of tomorrow will be capable of functioning in a new upcoming century of advance technology and competitive living, or to continue to allow public education in this country to decay.

The reform process in public education in this country requires a revolution - a revolution characterized by choices that bring about major changes. Each individual school and school system must be held accountable for providing quality learning outcomes to the students.

The foremost and major decision that must be made within each state in order to begin building a solid foundation of educational exellence within our public schools is to offer parents a free choice as to which

"Nobody likes change, but
business as usual in
the public education system
is going to put us out
of business ... A system
without incentives and
rewards drives out the good
and favors the mediocre."
--Albert Shanker,
President
American Federation of
Teachers

school they desire their children to attend. States like Minnesota, Iowa, and Arkansas have taken the stand in one form or another to support the choice plan. Some twenty states are currently taking a serious look at the choice plan. Such an approach has the basic ingredient of providing accountability through competition. I believe that competition among our public schools is the much needed force that will improve our public education system in this country. Only through the process of competition among schools within the same district, as well as between other districts, will public education begin to achieve its full potential. There should be no excuses why student test scores cannot improve in every school throughout this country.

Alan McGinnis, author of Bringing Out the Best in People (1985), illustrates the value of competition. McGinnis relates the following story of Charles Schwab who was general supervisor of Andrew Carnegie's steel mills.

> One day a particular mill manager was relating to Schwab what he had done to get his men to make their quota of work. "I've coaxed the men, I've pushed them, I've threatened them with damnation and being fired," the manager told Schwab, "but nothing works. They just won't produce."......
>
> "Give me a piece of chalk," Schwab said. Then turning to the nearest man he asked, "How many heats did your shift make today?"
>
> "Six."
>
> Without another word, Schwab chalked a big figure 6 on the floor and walked away.
>
> When the night shift came in they saw the 6 and asked what it meant. "The big boss was in here today," the day men said, "and chalked on the floor the number of heats we made."

The next morning Schwab walked through
the mill again. The night shift had
rubbed out the 6 and replaced it with a
big 7. When the day shift reported for
work the next morning, they saw the big
7 chalked on the floor. "So the night
shift thought they were better than the
day shift, did they?" Well, they would
show them a thing or two. The men
pitched in with enthusiasm and when they
quit that night, they left behind them
an enormous, swaggering 10.

Shortly, this mill which had been
lagging way behind in production was
turning out more work than any other
mill in the industry. And what was the
principle? Here is Schwab's description
of it.

"The way to get things done is to
stimulate competition. I do not mean in
a sordid, money-getting way, but in the
desire to excel."

Let me pose two questions as a parent. Are there
some schools in the local school system that you would
prefer to have your child attend or not attend? Could
you explain your reasons for selecting one school over
the others? Now suppose I would explain to you that in
the choice plan the following outcomes would occur:

1. There would be improved performance
   of paid professionals through
   competition.

2. Marketing of the product (education)
   would be ongoing.

3. Principals and teachers would become
   more accountable to the public
   (stockholders).

4. Colleges and universities would be
   forced to improve their training of
   school administrators and teachers as

graduates would compete with those
graduating from quality institutions.

5. School boards would become closer
aligned to the needs of the total
community, and cooperation would
increase between board members and
total district personnel since
division and split-voting over school
issues would serve to drive the
parents and their children to other
schools in other school districts.

6. Evaluation of personnel would become
more individualized based on annual
asssessment of district and school
priorities with continued emphasis
being directed towards increasing
student achievement and providing a
much improved climate for learning to
take place.

7. Creativity would flourish in classroom scheduling, curriculum and
instructional development, and
professional development since
emphasis would be on excellence and
achieving desired outcomes.

8. If applicable, the issue of
desegregation would be addressed.

9. Financing of education in the school
district would be distributed among
schools based on enrollments and
local effort with merit bonuses
offered to those teachers and
administrators who excel.

10. Professionalism would increase among
teachers and administrators based on
competition and recognition.

11. Evaluation of programs and
instruction in schools would be on
going in order to substantiate

existence to the general education
community.

12. Research work at higher education
institutions would take on a greater
significance originating from demands
of the practitioners in the field who
desire answers to program
developments and instructional
planning.

Now, would you be excited about a reform movement
that not only provided parental choice in public
schools but, at the same time, created total improvement in the operation of our public education system?
The parents' free choice plan of selecting schools
would create the driving force behind the improvement
of public education in this country at all levels. The
process would support many of the recommended choices
that need to be made in the operation of public education in this country that were suggested in each of the
preceding chapters. Local school districts that are
held accountable for turning out a marketable educational product would require competent administrators
and teachers. Therefore, educational training institutions would then be forced into either choosing to
improve their training programs and staying in business
or continuing along the same path of graduating a
product of mediocrity soon to discover that such a
choice puts them out of business.

School boards controlled by radical special-
interest groups characterized by leadership dissension,
for example, would not last long under the parent free-
choice plan since parents would opt to send their
children to school districts that have chosen to have a
well-managed organization.

Therefore, the concept of free choice of schools
based on competition will result in the "rippling
effect" of improving public education in this country
at all levels.

Would you choose and support an educational system
that hit the target relating to implementing action
based improvements? Would you support an educational

"It is through schools that
the nation has chosen to
pursue enlightened ends
for all its people and
it is here that the battle
for the future of America
will be won or lost."
--<u>An Imperiled Generation</u>
The Carnegie Foundation
Special Report

plan that was low on procrastination and high on
action? Would you care to have bureaucratic red tape
drastically reduced in schools so that principals can
manage effectively and teachers are free to actually
teach and work individually with high risk students?
Would you prefer to have a school where students are
excited about their school and they have a sense of
pride? Sure you would, and so would countless others
in this country because this is what every parent and
supporter of public education has been wanting for
years. They want schools that work.

The choice to have our schools working in this
country is no small undertaking. However, deciding to
do so must first begin at the doorstep of every local
elementary and secondary public school in this country.
It is at the local level of public education where we
as parents deposit our children trusting they will
acquire a growing interest in their education resulting
in future achievement. The bottom line for the total
educational community is deciding (1) what choices are
available once the critical issues are presented and
(2) whether selecting a certain route will result in
what's best for the students? Educational quality in
this country has been simmering on the back burner for
years but never really cooking to the extent it was
worth serving. For example, in this country one adult
in five is functionally illiterate. Compare such a
figure with Japan where there is general literacy.
This area has to be addressed in public education.
There can be no more dragging the feet on this one!

The need for accountability through competition is
long overdue in making our schools productive. Parents
who know in advance the educational outcomes of a
school are in a much better position, given the opportunity, to wisely select the proper school for their
son's or daughter's educations. They will know whether
or not a school is achieving what it is supposed to
achieve. They will know that curriculum includes
topics that need to be taught. They will also know the
dropout rate for each school and what is being done to
keep students in schools since recent studies show that
one-third of America's forty million students are
potential dropout victims. They will also know what is
being done to address marginal teaching and teacher

incompetency.

The majority of reform reports have taken the approach that, in order to improve public education in this country, we need more specialized programs where students are pulled out of the regular classroom and sent to a special class for instruction. We currently have students running all over school. They no more get to social studies class than they must go to the remediation room for math or the advance room for fine arts. This results in total fragmentation of the student's educational program, not to mention the disruption it causes in the classroom. Very little evaluation is going on to judge whether pull-out programs are working. In addition to pull-out programs, we have alternative schools, sex education, gifted instruction, driver education, bi-lingual instruction and "you name it" study programs, just to name a few. What is happening is that we are overloading the educational circuit in our schools.

It is also important to remember that within our present system of assigning students to schools based on boundary areas, there are no two schools alike. Management personalities differ; socio-economic levels vary; and parent support or lack of support exists. This means that within the framework of any school district the individual schools contain many unique differences. Disciplinary procedures may vary widely from school to school; teacher evaluations equally show degrees of variation within the same school district; and the total management process regarding district policies and procedures, although equally applying to all the schools, will show varying degrees of enforcement and adherance.

So, the plan of offering free choice to parents as to what school they wish to send their children is a revolutionary movement that must occur if we are to improve public education in this country. Certainly those schools and school districts that are achieving desired outcomes will attract interested parents.

The revolution I am suggesting is not an overthrow of our present system of public education. The values and tradition upon which the foundation of free educa-

tion was built in this country must be preserved.
However, the urgent need to address the low pay of
administrators and teachers, school dropouts, falling
test scores, declining interest in science and mathematics, teenage gangs, sub-par professional training
programs, school board division, lack of administrative
leadership, bureaucracy, political intrusion, and
special self-interest groups cannot be dealt with
effectively through ad hoc committee reports regardless
of whether they are labeled as blue, red, or yellow
ribbon committees. We simply don't need to waste taxpayer dollars to do another study on what is wrong with
public education in this country. The need is for
reform with action.

The Nation at Risk report on public education in
this country and the reports that have followed served
a purpose. They brought the need for change in our
public schools to our attention. Many were alarmed
after reading and hearing what was happening inside of
our elementary and secondary schools. State legislatures responded by cranking out mandates directed
primarily towards local school districts to improve the
education of children, which carried high price tags
with minimum state support. All kinds of educational
requirement packages have been shooting out of the
bureaucratic cannons since the mid-1980's. The requirement packages have included teacher competency
tests, administrator/teacher evaluation instruments,
student proficiency exams, merit pay, longer school
year, back to "the basics" instruction, and pass/play
requirements, to name a few. These and other requirements have a purpose and that is to improve the product
of education in our public school systems.

However, the concerns that I have are (1) testing
does not necessarily mean teaching is going on, (2) the
majority of reform packages treat administrative leadership as a low priority, and (3) the force behind the
need for change in our local schools is coming from the
federal and state levels and not at the local levels.
It is this author's belief that lasting change for the
better can only come about if autonomy and flexibility
are extended to local school districts so they might be
able to exercise leadership and management practices
that will enhance the achievement of the goal: Pro-

viding Educational Excellence in our Schools.

The choice plan will offer families greater autonomy in the governance of individual schools. It will also place greater emphasis on extensive evaluation and testing to indicate whether the schools are working or not working. At a recent gathering at the White House of invited educators and choice advocates, Joe Nathan, senior fellow at the Hubert Humphrey Institute of Public Affairs, stated: "Choice by itself will not solve all of our problems, but it permits the freedom educators want and the opportunities students need, while encouraging the dynamism that our public education system requires" (Snider, Education Week, 18 January 1989, p. 24).

The American taxpayers will pay one way or another. We will pay for prisons for uneducated dropouts who steal for a living. We will pay for teenagers who refuse to achieve. We might as well pay for quality education. It will be less taxing on us all in the long run. Whether the funding comes from state or federal treasuries, it must be allocated to local school districts without strings attached so that local school boards can determine how it should be spent to achieve desired outcomes. Additional funding must continue to school districts that have specialized programs. What public schools can and must do is to teach kids and teach them effectively with emphasis on turning out a quality product based on individual needs and abilities. The responsibility of educating our youth must be returned to the local level. With some 15,300 local school districts in this country, the idea of such a revolutionary reform movement presents a host of challenges. But as we know from past history, the great revolutionary reform movement that brought our country our freedom and growth will continue to be faced with tremendous challenges as we move into a new century. Regardless of the magnitude of the challenges of the 21st century, we must remember that the problems we may face can be dealt with if we have educated our children properly. The mission of changing mountains into super highways within our public education system throughout this country must be put to contract, signed, sealed, and delivered to each local school agency.

John T. Goodlad in his book, <u>A Place Called</u>
<u>School,</u> commented on the question, "Can we have effec-
tive schools?" He put it this way.

> To the extent that the attainment of a
> democratic society depends on the
> existence of schools equally accessible
> to everyone, we are all their clients.
> It is not easy, however, to convince a
> majority of our citizens that this
> relationship exists and that schools
> require their support because of it. It
> is especially difficult to convince them
> if they perceive the schools to be
> deficient in regard to their traditional
> functions. Unfortunately, the ability
> of schools to do their traditional jobs
> of assuring literacy and eradicating
> ignorance is at the center of current
> criticism, which is intense.

I have attempted to offer a road of reform in
public education that will lead to progress as we head
into the 21st century. What our children know and
don't know will affect everyone. The choice plan of
reform through competition at the local school level
has all the ingredients that will sustain and improve
public education as we look towards the 21st century.
The time to act is now while public education and the
need to reform is at the top of the list.

Making the choice to forge ahead with pioneering
efforts to address the substantial challenges that face
American public schools will bring about desired outcomes. Choosing to maintain the status quo, continuing
to be satisfied with mediocrity and complacency in our
public schools will definitely curtail our growth
within the international market of achievement as we
prepare to enter into the 21st century.

I have stated that the journey towards excellence
in our schools contains an abundance of challenges
which must be addressed if our destination of reforming
public education in this country is to be reached.
Challenges along the way must be treated as simply a
junction in the road. We cannot head into the 21st

century with dead-end streets in public education. Choices: Public Education for the 21st Century has been an honest attempt by this author to affirm our precious heritage of public education in this country and, at the same time, offer the choices that must be made to advance this heritage.

"Leaders have a significant role in creating the state of mind that is society. They can serve as symbols of the moral unity of the society. They can express the values that hold society together. Most important, they can conceive and articulate goals that lift people out of their petty preoccupations, carry them above the conflicts that tear a society apart and unite them in the pursuit of objectives worthy of their best efforts."

--John Gardner

References

Adizes, Ichak. How to Solve the Mismanagement Crisis. San Diego: Adizes Institute, 1981.

An Evaluation Instrument for Assessing Board of Education Effectiveness and Superintendent's Performance. Introduction taken from Becoming a Better Board Member. Aurora Public Schools, District 131, Aurora, Illinois, March 1983.

"Annual Average Industry and Occupation Tables for Year Ending December, 1986 (Table 35)." Employed Persons by Detailed Industry and Major Occuptions. Published by Bureau of Labor Statistics.

"Big Cities Try to Define Good Teachers, Administrators." Education U.S.A. eds. National School Public Relations Association, Washington, D.C., 9 April 1979, p. 241.

Blanchard, Kenneth, and Spencer Johnson. The One Minute Manager. New York: Berkley Books, 1983.

Bok, Derek. The President's Report 1985-86, Harvard University. April 1987.

Broadley, Margaret E. "The Teacher." Your Natural Gifts. McLean, VA: EPM Publications, Inc., 1977, p. 61-68.

Brookover, William, and Larry Lezatte. The Effective School: School Climate. Jackson, Mississippi: Kelwynn Group, 1984 (An Effective School's Learning Album).

"Bulletin Board: Positions Available." Chronicle of Higher Education. 12 September 1984, pp. 44-71;

26 September 1984, pp. 42-71; 21 November 1984, pp. 38-71.

Cawelti, Gordon. "Guess What? Big City Superintendents Say Their School Boards Are Splendid." The
American School Board Journal. March 1982, pp.
33-35.

"Changing Course: A Fifty-State Survey of Reform
Measures." Education Week. 6 February 1985, pp.
11, 30.

Chase, Clinton. How to Get an 'A': Be Neat, Be First,
Change Your Name.

Cohen, Deborah. "California City, District Forge Pack
on Use of Schools." Education Week. 3 May 1989,
p. 4.

"Colleges Rated on Education Research." Education
Week. 27 April 1983, p. 3.

"Curriculum Leadership." Challenges for School Leaders. Arlington: American Association of School
Administrators, 1988.

Danzberger, Jacqueline, et.al. "School Boards, The
Forgotten Players on the Education Team." Phi
Delta Kappan. September 1987, pp. 59-60.

Data-Search: Estimates of School Statistics--1988-89.
eds. National Education Association, 1989.

Educators Newsletter. Published by Northern Illinois
Gas. eds. The National Research Bureau, Inc.,
Washington, D.C., and Burlington, Iowa, February
1981, p. 3.

Elam, Stanley M. "Second Gallup Phi Delta Kappan Poll
of Teachers' Attitudes Toward the Public Schools."
Phi Delta Kappan. June 1989, p. 790.

"Enrollment Swells in Private Schools." Chicago
Tribune. 20 December 1984.

"Excellence Recommendations: Keys to Reform?" School

Board News. 30 November 1983, p. 8.

Foster Susan G. "Schools of Education Are Urged to Promote Global Awareness." Education Week. 7 December 1981, p. 6.

Fuhr, Don. "Selecting First Year Teachers." Bulletin. ed. National Association of Secondary Principals. February 1977, pp. 57-59.

Fuhr, Don. "Ten Best Ways to Kill Leadership." The School Administrator. September 1988, pp. 50-51.

Gallup, Alec M., and Stanley M. Elam. "The Twentieth Annual Gallup Poll of the Public's Attitudes Toward the Public Schools." Phi Delta Kappan. September 1988, p. 33-46.

"Get the Community on the School Team." Building Confidence in Our Schools. ed. American Association of School Administrators, 1983.

Goldberg, Kirsten. "Private Schools and Reform: E.D. Conferences Urge a Collaboration." Education Week. 2 November 1988, p. 24.

Goodlad, John T. "Can We Have Effective Schools?" A Place Called School. New York: McGraw Hill Book Company, 1984, p. 2.

Greenberger, Robert. Public Schools: Still the American Melting Pot.

Griffin, Jean Latz. "Union Chief Exhorts Teachers to Reform." Chicago Tribune, 1984.

Hammond, Linda Darling. Beyond the Commission Reports: The Coming Crisis in Education. A review taken from Rand Checklist. June 1988, pp. 10-11.

Haderlein, Robert V. "Strengthen the Leadership Team." The American School Board Journal. October 1981, p. 50.

Heller, Robert W., et.al. Here's Your Blunt Critique of Administrator Preparation." The Executive

Educator. September 1988, pp. 18-21, 30.

Hillkirk, John. "Execs Focus on Resurrecting Education." U.S.A. Today. 3 February 1989, Sec. B, p. 1.

Hodgkinson, Harold L. "What's Ahead for Education." Principal. January 1986, pp. 6-11.

Holding Effective Board Meetings. ed. American Association of School Administrators and the National School Boards Association. Arlington: American Association of School Administrators, 1984.

Jackson, Philip. "Today's Teachers Are Better." Instructor. January 1975, pp. 46-47.

Jennings, Lisa. "New Jersey Plan Widens Access to Principalship." Education Week. 14 September 1988, pp. 1, 13.

Kimbrough, Ralph B., and Michael Y. Nunnery. "The Tasks of Educational Administration." Educational Administration: An Introduction. New York: Macmillan Publishing Company, 1988, pp. 44-80.

Kipp, David F. "But These Board Members Drive Superintendents Crazy." The American School Board Journal. March 1982, p. 35.

"Letters to the Editor: Isabel E. Carpio." The Beacon News.

Levering, Robert, et.al. "Introduction: Beyond Technique." The 100 Best Companies to Work for in America. Reading, Massachusetts: Addison-Wesley Publishing Co., 1984.

Louv, Richard. "Hard Time for Students." Seneca Journal Tribune. 20 August 1988, p. 4.

Madaus, George, and Diana Pullin. "Teacher Certification Tests: Do They Really Measure What We Need to Know?" Phi Delta Kappan. September 1987, pp. 31-38.

Mamchak, Susan and Steven R. School Administrator's Public Speaking Portfolio. West Nyack, N.Y.: Parker Publishing Co., Inc., 1983, pp. 189-90.

Marling, William. "The Clothes Make the Man, If the Man Knows John Molloy." Pastimes. August 1975, pp. 14-17, 25, 27.

McGinnis, Alan Loy. "The Will to Win." Bringing Out the Best in People. Minneapolis: Augusburg Publishing House, 1985, pp. 126-135.

"Michigan Study Reveals Why Superintendents Get Fired." Information Legislative Service. ed. Pennsylvania School Boards Association. 6 August 1976, pp. 1-3.

Motivational Quotes. Lombard, Illinois: Great Quotations, Inc., 1984.

Nation At Risk, A. ed. The National Commission on Excellence in Education, April 1983, p. 22.

"1989 Back-to-School Forecast." News. ed. United States Department of Education, 24 August 1989.

O'Brien, Robert. Marriott: The J. Willard Marriott Story. Salt Lake City: Deseret Book Company, 1987.

Olds, Robert. "Study Produces Painful Insights about Why Some Superintendents Come Untracked." Illinois School Board Journal. November-December 1980, pp. 20-21.

Peck, M. Scott. The Road Less Traveled. New York: Simon and Schuster, 1978.

"People: Grant Colfax." Education Week. 14 September 1983.

Peters, Thomas J., and Robert H. Waterman, Jr. In Search of Excellence, New York: Harper and Row, 1982.

Presenting Good Spellers. Allen Elementary School,

Aurora, Illinois, 11 May 1981.

"Profile of SAT's and Achievement Test Taking."
National Report, College Board College Bound
Seniors, 1988. pp. III, 8.

Providence-St. Mel High School.   Investing in a
Miracle. 1983-84.

"Reform, Scores Are Stagnating, Cavazos Warns."
Leadership News. 15 May 1989, pp. 1, 8.

Ryan, Michael.   "The Man Who Shapes Up Troubled
Schools." Parade Magazine. 3 September 1989, pp.
18-21.

Rothman, Robert.   "A Town and Gown Reform."   Education
Week. 7 September 1988, pp. 1, 16.

Rothman, Robert.   "Carnegie 'Units' Should Go, Says
Study by Boards." Education Week. 2 November
1988, pp. 1, 18.

Rowson, Joseph.   "Coping with Alinskey Methods."   The
School Administrator. March 1983, pp. 23-25.

"Sage Advice on Superintendent-Board Relationship."
Information Legislative Service. ed. Pennsylvania
School Boards Association. 6 August 1976, p. 3.

Schneider, Barbara, et.al.   "The Deans' Perspective on
the Status of Doctoral Programs in Schools of
Education." Phi Delta Kappan.   May 1984, pp.
617-620.

Silberman, Charles E.   Crisis in the Classroom.   New
York: Random House, 1970.

Silberman, Charles E.   "The Education of Educators."
Crisis in the Classroom. New York: Random House,
1970, pp. 472-73.

Snider, William.   "Parley on 'Choice,' Final Budget
Mark Transition." Education Week.   17 January
1989, pp. 1, 24.

"State, Local School Chiefs Ranked among Best-Paid Public Officials." Education Week. 7 September 1988, p. 13.

Strother, Deborah Burnett. "Latchkey Children: The Fastest-Growing Special Interest Group in the Schools." Phi Delta Kappan. June 1989, p. 290.

"Study: Poor Teachers Get Free Ride." Beacon-News. 12 August 1984, Sec. A., p. 13.

"Teaching Revolution: Rochester at Front of Crusade, A." Greenville News. 31 January 1988, Sec. E, p. 1.

"375, 4400 or Fight." AASA Convention Reporter. 13 February 1981, p. 7.

Toffler, Alvin. Future Shock. New York: Random House, 1970.

To Save Our Schools, To Save Our Children. ABC Television, 4 September 1984.

"12% of Teens Using Drugs and Alcohol." Chicago Tribune. 8 September 1984, Sec. 1, p. 2.

Vejnoska, Jill. "Youngsters Are Getting Fatter, Not Fitter." U.S.A. Today. 15-17 September 1989, pp. 1A, 8C.

"Virginia Teachers List Moral Support as Priority." Education U.S.A. eds. National School Public Relations Association, Washington, D.C. 16 June 1980, p. 318.

Walton, Susan. "'There Are No One-Two-Three Solutions' for Schools' Problems." Education Week. 23 November 1983, pp. 12, 15.

Weil, Nellie C. "The Significance of Being a School Board Member." American School Boards: The Positive Power. Alexandria: National School Boards Association, 1987.

West, Peter. "IBM will Earmark $25 Million in Grants

for School Activities." Education Week. 10 May 1989, p. 1.

Wing, R. L. "Illusion and Reality." The Art of Strategy. New York: Doubleday, 1988, p. 81.

Wise, Arthur E., and Linda Darling-Hammond. Teacher Evaluation: A Study of Effective Practices. A review taken from Rand Checklist. June 1988, p. 11.

Wynn, Richard, and Charles W. Guditus. "Leadership." Team Management: Leadership by Consensus. Columbus: Charles Merrill Publishing Co., 1984, p. 35.

Zigler, Zig. "Characteristics of Goals." See You at the Top. Gretna, Louisiana: Pelican Publishing Co., Inc., 1987, p. 165.

About the Author

Don Fuhr has served as a senior level executive for school districts in Ohio, Pennsylvania, and Illinois. He has received recognition from many educational and community groups for his ability to motivate administrators, teachers, students, and communities. He has "been there" (in the trenches); he "is there" currently working with graduate students in educational administration at Clemson University which puts him inside public schools nearly every day of the week. As a mentor/consultant, Don Fuhr provides practical and stimulating guidelines for his students, colleagues, and readers through speeches and seminar presentations throughout the country.

His combined skills and ideas have enabled him to not only set high goals, but also to motivate others to attain goals through persistence and teamwork. He is the author of a variety of articles focusing on leadership and general school management which have appeared in professional journals and periodicals of state and national organizations.

The book, Choices: Public Education for the 21st Century, relates many of the author's challenging experiences as a frontline public school administrator and identifies what choices need to be made at all levels in order to propel public education in this country towards greater heights.